Values from the Front Porch

Remembering the Wisdom of Our Grandmothers

Jane Middelton-Moz

Health Communications, Inc.
Deerfield Beach, Florida

www.hcibooks.com

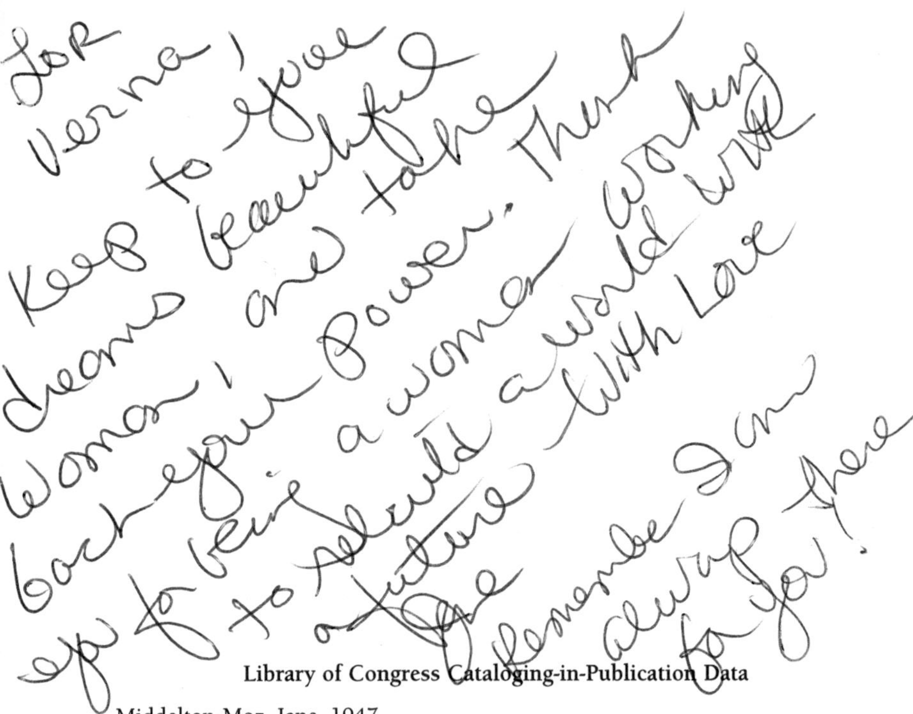

Library of Congress Cataloging-in-Publication Data

Middelton-Moz, Jane, 1947

Values from the front porch : remembering the wisdom of our grandmothers / Jane Middelton-Moz.

p. cm.

ISBN 0-7573-0297-1

1. Grandmothers—Anecdotes. 2. Values. 3. Conduct of life. 4. Moral education. I. Title.

HQ759.9.M53 2006
306.874'5—dc22

2005044739

ISBN 0-7573-0297-1

Publisher: Health Communications, Inc.
3201 S.W. 15th Street
Deerfield Beach, FL 33442-8190

Cover design by Andrea Perrine Brower
Inside book design by Lawna Patterson Oldfield

This book is dedicated to the grandmothers in all of our lives who have given us the priceless gifts of their love, wisdom and values. I wish to express my respect for and appreciation of the grandmothers whose values have been shared in this book:

Jeannie Angnatuk
Lily Berger
Mary Edwards
Lois Frederica Fordham
Florence Glassmire
Margaret Goble
Ida Goodleaf (Kawennotie)
Lola Gertrude Harrmann
Mary Lou Hudson
Jean Jeffries
Lillian Johnson
Itoe Kawamoto
Eva Lane
Diane Margaret Laut
Eileen Moyes
Katerina Cassatorie Panzica
Mary Louise James Rapada
Hazel Inez Jules Salle
Mary Jane Thomas
Corinne Chapin Titus
Marjorie Valier
Jessie Wartinbee
Faye Avidon Weiss
Bertha Leaver Whatmough
Susie Chief Williams (Alimpa?ay)

CONTENTS

FOREWORD

I like to walk with Grandma, her steps
are short like mine. She never says, "Now hurry up!"
She always takes her time. I like to walk with
Grandma, her eyes see things like mine do, wee pebbles
bright, a funny cloud, half-hidden drops of dew.
Most people have to hurry. They do not stop
and see. I'm so glad that God made Grandma,
unrushed and young like me.

—AUTHOR UNKNOWN

Three things inspired me to write this book. First, I received a number of letters from children while writing *Welcoming Our Children to the New Millennium*. They told me that they fear living in a world without values, and that they want adults to model and teach them. One young girl went so far as to suggest that if adults want children and youth to begin acting more responsibly, they need grandparents in every living room. She said that in most living rooms the TV set is the "elder" teaching children values today.

The next inspiration came when I was having coffee with friends.

One friend's grandmother had died six months before, and he was still grieving the loss. "I am a lucky man," he said. "I received tradition and a priceless inheritance of values from my grandmother. She was devoted to her grandchildren and always told us stories, but I would realize only years later that these stories had life lessons buried within them. She shared her experiences, convictions and opinions, and always told me she loved me at the end of every conversation." Another friend spoke up, "My grandmother and I would have our best conversations when we were peeling potatoes, making jam, sharing a meal or taking a walk. She taught me the values I live by today. She also taught me to dance, and I learned some of my favorite songs from my granny."

A third friend remained silent and seemed sad. When I asked her if she was all right, she replied, "I really feel ripped off. I didn't have a grandmother who taught me values. My grandmothers died before I was born; it makes me sad not to have had a grandmother in my life. I love to hear your stories though. In a way I feel like I'm sharing all your grandmothers' teachings by just listening to you.

My third inspiration came after I read an article summarizing the findings of several research studies on the effect of grandparents in the lives of children and youth. The research clearly showed that grandparents are the reservoirs of family wisdom, role models who demonstrate how to deal with the world outside of home and mentors who teach children ways of working with the basic materials of life. A 2002 study reported that 66.7 percent of college students surveyed said that they received support from their grandmothers. The study indicated that grandmothers taught their grandchildren the values they lived by. In addition, 63.4 percent of the college students surveyed said their grandmothers provided them with guidance, had regular social interactions with them and talked about the personal concerns of their lives. These interactions were characteristic of the grandparent-grandchild relationship they enjoyed (Block 2002).

Values are beliefs and attitudes about what is good, right, desirable and worthwhile in the world. They are internal convictions that support our movement through life, our relationships with others and, ultimately, our relationship with ourselves. Values are not prescribed or imposed rules, but rather beliefs that are cultivated inside us by role models in our lives. Our value systems are like maps in our hearts that give us direction for our judgments and choices. Our values allow us to find our way during some of the most confusing and uncertain times in our lives.

Many people who do not have a well-formed value system are confused, not knowing what is right or just. They have no inner compass to guide them, so they make decisions based only on what they can see; they seek happiness where it cannot be found; they are driven by the reactions of others.

Grandmothers teach us valuable lessons about life and provide a sympathetic ear, mentoring, love and direction during some of our most difficult and confusing times of life. Unfortunately, most of us can't run next door to seek the wisdom of a grandparent. Gone are the days when generations lived within a few blocks of each other. In this book, twenty-three grandmothers share their warmth, wisdom and values that have provided the firm foundations of their lives. Their stories teach basic lessons about life that have brought them peace, happiness, contentment and satisfaction.

HOW TO USE THIS BOOK

Values from the Front Porch: Remembering the Wisdom of Our Grandmothers is divided into twenty-three chapters. Each chapter explores a value, presents the story of a grandmother modeling the value and provides exercises that help to strengthen the value in one's life. Some readers will simply want to read about the value and the story, while others will also complete the exercises. I recommend that you purchase a journal, referred to as your "Values Journal," to do the exercises at the end of each chapter. Divide your journal into twenty-three sections, and label each section with the appropriate value. For example, the first section would be labeled Celebrating Life, the second Constancy, the third Respect and so forth. The exercises will direct you to write in the appropriate section of your journal. You may choose to go through this book with a friend or your family. You might start an adult or youth reading group, discussing the value and then doing the exercises together.

ACKNOWLEDGMENTS

The completion of this book allows me to honor and celebrate the gifts of many people without whom it never could have been written. I appreciate and thank all of you more than words can say.

I would like to offer a special acknowledgment and heartfelt thank-you to the caring and compassionate individuals who took the time to honor the wisdom, heart gifts and priceless memories of their grandmothers: Marissa Baker, Eleanor "Joy" Belmont, Keri Black-Deegan, Michele Avidon Brook, Carlie Chase, Georgine Dellisanti, Amy Louise Fordham, Suzy Goodleaf, Terry Harrmann, Sue Hawkins, Sarah Healy, Michele Hill, Rod Kawamoto, Cassie Kenworthy, Samuel Jeffries, Suzanne LaFleche, Jeff Lindholm, Jan Longboat, Doug Moyes, Theresa Peluso, Tammy and Terri Picard, Judy Piper, Annie Popert, Albert and Veronica Redstar, and Lisa Tener.

I would like to thank my children for their wisdom and loving support and for the unique gifts they have shared with me: Shawn, Jason, Damien and Forrest Lesch Middelton; Lisa Middelton; Sarah Healy; Melinda and Michael Knight; Suzy Goodleaf; and Diane Labelle.

My appreciation for their love, joyfulness, wisdom, and beautiful and unique spirits goes to my grandchildren: Logan, Canaan and

Anastasia Middelton; Ryan and Christopher Flannery; and Sage and Jamie Labelle-Goodleaf. You are the lights of my life.

For their love and support in completing this book, I offer heartfelt thanks to my brother and sister-in-law, Alex and Marena Ward, and to my nephew Edward Ward.

My sincere thanks go to Rod Jeffries, Wanda Gabriel, Shirley Walker, John R. Fletcher, Sarah Miller, Harold Belmont and Lizzie Epoh-York for their ideas, contributions and support in completing this book.

I appreciate more than I can possibly express the heart gifts of my friends and extended family, whose continual support and encouragement spurred me on and allowed me to complete this book: Elaine Lussier, Jimmy and Robin Nicholas, Vera Manuel, Christina and Stan Grof, Mary and Ken Carter, Jean Jacque Guyot, Jeannie May, Jackie Thomas, Mabel Louie, Ann Harrmann, Kim Sebastian, Bill Laut, Charlie Gordon, Mary Aitchison, Paul Ferland, Luke and John Jeffries, Mary Lee and Denny Zawadski, and Peaco Todd.

I would like to thank two beautiful grandmothers, Suzanne Smith and Lori Keip, for their much-appreciated kindness and support throughout the years and for their endless patience and energy.

I want to give a genuine thank-you to my extremely talented and supportive editor, Elisabeth Rinaldi. My deepest thanks for continued support, care and kindness go to Peter Vegso, Terry Burke, Lisa Drucker, Kim Weiss, Paola Fernandez, Susan Tobias, Larissa Henoch, Kelly Maragni, Lawna Patterson Oldfield, Dawn Von Strolley Grove and the entire staff of Health Communications, Inc.

I would also like to thank Roger Strauss and the staff of the Institute of Professional Practice for their time, energy, kindness and laughter and for being the wonderful supportive people they are.

Celebrating Life

Keep a green tree in your heart and perhaps
the singing bird will come.

—Chinese Proverb

On November 28, 2004, a chartered plane carrying Susan Saint James' family crashed upon takeoff. Her fourteen-year-old son, Edward Ebersol, was killed in the crash. In an interview several months later, Susan Saint James was asked if she was angry about the errors that might have caused the crash. She responded, "Holding on to resentments is like taking poison and hoping the other guy dies." Instead, she focused on her blessings: the fact that her husband and older son had been saved, the joy Edward's life had given her and all those who knew him, the heroism of her older son, and the outpouring of support her family had received from people throughout the world.

Many people suffer enormous trauma and loss in their lives, yet somehow grieve fully, let go of resentments, and enjoy and celebrate the gifts life offers. Others stay stuck in their feelings of victimization or guilt and hold on to lifelong resentments that slowly poison their lives and relationships, which can affect their physical and emotional health.

It isn't possible to live life without problems or some degree of suffering and grief. Yet there are those who focus their energy on unfairness or casting blame rather than seek a solution to their problems. The more we focus only on our problems, the bigger they become and the greater the likelihood that we miss seeing the gifts that enter our lives. A father might focus his energy on the unfairness that his neighbor has a new car and miss the joy of celebrating his child's first smile.

Early one morning a number of years ago, I was sitting on a bench in the beautiful garden of the hotel where I was staying. I was enjoying the beauty around me when an older man sat down beside me. "Ah, I so love the sounds of birds early in the morning and the sweet smell of flowers and freshly mown grass," he said, taking a deep breath.

As we talked, he told me about the diabetes that had robbed him of his sight, and I responded that it must have been difficult to lose his sight. He laughed, "Oh, yes, it was until the day I realized how fortunate I was to have discovered that my sense of smell and hearing became much more acute. You know, I used to take all this for granted," he said, gesturing to all that was around him. "For years I never smelled the grass nor heard the birds. In my loss, I have gained so much."

Later that morning, I was sitting in the restaurant of the same hotel. The couple at the next table spent their entire meal loudly complaining about the restaurant service, the laziness of the housekeeping staff, the temperature of the pool, the hardness of their mattress, the cost of their room and the weather. In fact, complaints were the sum total of their breakfast conversation.

The lesson I learned that day couldn't have been more obvious: celebration of life is not dependent on what has been received, nor is suffering always the outcome of what has been lost. Some people continually focus on what is *not*, whereas others live their lives celebrating what *is*.

Celebrating life isn't only allowing joyfulness, but it is also embracing loss, grieving fully, then letting go, all the while learning the lessons that both joy and sorrow have to teach. Loss is not optional in life; yet how we face loss, problems and suffering is a crucial element in determining the quality of our lives. Opening ourselves to joy and celebration is a priceless gift we give ourselves and our children.

"Muti"
Lily Berger

Today a new sun rises for me; everything lives, everything is animated, everything seems to speak to me of my passion, everything invites me to cherish it. . . .

—ANNE DE LENCLOS

Five-year-old Lily joyfully splashed in the water, celebrating her birthday and her brand new patent leather shoes. She loved walking through the stream by her uncle's house. She was enjoying herself so much that she didn't stop to think that her mother might be angry at the damage she was doing to her new shoes. She loved life and celebrated every part of it until the day she died.

Her blue eyes sparkling, Lily loved to tell her grandchildren stories of her life in Austria: the music, feasts, dancing and the lambs that would come only to her on her uncle's farm. "Grandma loved to tell us stories," her granddaughter Lisa said. "She told us about living in Vienna as a young girl. Her mother would invite all the young people to her home on Wednesday night. They would all bring their musical instruments and play late into the night; then they would all walk to a café, eat together and talk until the wee hours of the morning. Grandma loved music, playing the piano and dancing."

Celebrations, family and roots were vital to Lily. She was the one who laid a firm foundation, created a safe haven and demonstrated

---

The story of Lily Berger is based on an interview with her granddaughter Lisa Tener. Lisa is a published author and book coach who helps people bring their books to life. She thanks her Grandmother Lily for helping her believe in herself and her gifts. Lisa's Web site is www.LisaTener.com.

joy for her family, despite all that she had gone through as a child and all she had lost as a young woman.

Lily was born in Vienna, Austria, on October 17, 1906. She loved Vienna but was often sent to the country to visit her uncle and cousins when she was a small child. Although under the guise of "fattening her up," it was more likely that her parents sent her to the country so that she could be farther away from the war that was blazing through Europe. World War I cost Austria thousands of lives, including Lily's father's.

On the eve of World War II, the Nazis invaded Austria. Austrian Jews were forbidden to work, but the owners of the soap factory that Lily's husband, a highly respected perfume chemist, managed ignored the law and allowed him to continue his work. But one day the Gestapo came to Lily's home looking for her Jewish husband. Lily never lied, and in this case it was her undoing. She told the secret police that her husband was at work. He was arrested there, and by the end of the day he was imprisoned and was later sent to Dachau concentration camp.

Several things worked in Lily and her husband's favor, however. Early on, he had seen the handwriting on the wall and had put their names on a list to immigrate to the United States; the Nazis had not yet implemented the "final solution" at Dachau; and an influential family friend was able to get Lily's husband released from the concentration camp. He and Lily were then able to immigrate to Brooklyn as planned. Unfortunately, the rest of Lily's family realized too late the seriousness of Austria's political situation and were not allowed to leave the country. Her family died in Treblinka at the hands of the Nazis.

"I remember hearing the story about the day my grandmother received a letter from the Red Cross telling her of the deaths of her mother and sisters in the camp. She was overcome with grief, and my mother's older sister, Aunt Anne, who was really small then, put her arms around her mother, promising that she would never let her die," Lisa said tearfully. "The horrible inhumanity was too much for Grandma, yet in order to live her life and celebrate it as she always had, she somehow was able to grieve, then put the pain behind her, grateful for her safety and the safety of her husband and children."

Rather than feel continued bitterness about all she had lost, Lily focused on what she had. This incredible ability to celebrate life was passed on to her children and grandchildren. To Lily, everything was a celebration of life and family. There were celebrations of every holiday: Jewish New Year, Thanksgiving, birthdays, even Christmas. There were always lots of people, food and laughter filling Lily's grandchildren's young lives. "We had a German shepherd and Grandma even celebrated the dog's birthday. We'd eat the cake, and the dog would eat the ice cream," Lisa laughed.

Lily celebrated every achievement, milestone or rite of passage of her children, then grandchildren. There was always a party with lots of food. She would ask her grandchildren to perform again and again the childhood plays they created, and Lily applauded loudly each time. "She always celebrated our achievements no matter how small. I will never forget the black-and-white television she bought me and the party she gave when I got my first period," Lisa laughed.

Lily had a big house that she shared with Lisa and her family. She also rented out a room, usually to someone who had just come to the United States from Europe. Everyone who rented the room ended up calling Lily "Muti" (Yiddish for "grandmother"), although Lisa's family and friends called Lily "Grandma." "She attracted people to her because of her joyfulness," Lisa said. "She sparkled and had a genuinely open heart. What amazed me about my grandma was that she'd come to the United States with her husband and baby, all her family left behind, yet was able to create a strong family for her children and grandchildren with a firm foundation of tradition, safety, security and values. She had a life force inside her that was special to everyone who met her."

Lily Berger died the way she lived, celebrating life and family. Very sick and close to death, Lily had already said good-bye to her family. Every movement and word was an effort for her. Yet when her granddaughter Diana made a zucchini casserole for her, she rallied once again. "Because she always celebrated our every accomplishment, she asked us to bring her from the bed to the chair so she could eat some of the casserole, as sick as she was," Lisa said. "She took a few small bites and spoke very slowly, every word labored. It seemed to take forever to get the sentence out. "I have just one thing to say; that zucchini casserole was terrific!"

"Later that day, my sister and mother got into an argument over how to get someplace. My grandmother told a joke that broke the tension and made us all laugh. She was so good at that, even when she had so little breath to speak."

Lisa feels that her grandmother's joyful spirit will be with her for the rest of her life. "Her presence gives me faith that spurs me on. Her laughter, open heart and joyful celebration of life are inside me, guiding me in everything I do."

Celebrating Life Consciously

When one door of happiness closes, another opens;
but often we look so long at the closed door that we do not
see the one which has been opened to us.

—Helen Keller

Start Each Day Intentionally

- Begin each day by focusing on how you would like the day to be and what you need to put into the day to make it that way. Think of things that may be important for you to celebrate today: your child's first day of school, trying a new recipe, the first day of spring. Ask yourself how you will celebrate today. Write down your intention for the day in the Celebrating Life section of your "Values Journal."
- At the end of the day, evaluate it. Has it gone the way you desired? If so, celebrate! (Take a bath, using candlelight and music; play your guitar; take a walk; enjoy the garden in the moonlight; or dance around the room with abandon. Do whatever pleases you.)

  If things didn't go as you intended, focus on what can you learn from today, which will be gifts of understanding for the future. Were there losses, conflicts or disappointments that you will carry into future days? Did you solve your problems, or did you make them bigger?

Journal Active Problems and Let Them Go

- Write in the Celebrating Life section of your "Values Journal" every night about current problems you are experiencing and attempted solutions that may not be working. For instance, you have a friend who is putting you down, and your solution has been to ignore her words. Ask yourself if ignoring her criticism is working. Cross off the failed solution, and write another solution that you feel might work. Eleanor Roosevelt once said, "No one can make you feel bad about yourself without your consent." Always put your journal away before going to sleep. Continually focusing on problems only makes them bigger. Sometimes allowing a bit of distance helps. Once you have resolved each problem, add the lessons you've learned to the Thankfulness section of your journal, and find a way to celebrate.

Take Time to Celebrate

- Celebration is an important part of everyday life. Whether it is celebrating a child's passage into adulthood, taking notice of the first snowfall of the season or celebrating the completion of your first quilt, don't let opportunities for celebration pass you by. We often become so caught up in schedules or problems that we bypass special things in our lives. Become aware of at least one thing each week worthy of celebration. Find creative ways to mark those important times in your life and in the lives of your loved ones.

Constancy

I cut out my wedding dress at the same place where I memorized my spelling words. It was in the same place that I ate Archway cookies every day after school. And it was there that I prepared for my SAT. My husband-to-be was grilled mercilessly in that same spot. Much of what I have learned and hold dear is inextricably intertwined with the kitchen table. . . . it was a key to the life I now have.

—Marianne Jennings

A number of years ago, I was in Europe on a business trip. On our way home, my late husband, Rudy, and I spent a few days in Florence, Italy. One day, while leisurely walking down a narrow street, I saw a craftsman high on scaffolding carefully repairing a small place where a piece of masonry had broken off. I thought, "How amazing to be in a place of such history! How amazing to have this kind of constancy surrounding you generation after generation." I was humbled by the care and love that had gone into the restoration of these beautiful buildings over hundreds of years. I thought of the small house that I had lived in as a young child, long since torn down, and of the human affection, care and constancy that is so important in forming the foundation of children's lives and the security in adult relationships. "How wonderful it would be," I thought at that moment, "if we put the same energy into lovingly tending our relationships with our children, significant others and friends that generations of craftsmen have put into these beautiful and ancient buildings—even those relationships that seem to be beyond repair."

Constancy according to the *American Heritage Dictionary* is defined as "steadfastness, as in purpose or affection, faithfulness, changelessness." It may be one of the most important values that generations of loving grandmothers have provided in building and gently repairing the solid foundations of our lives. Empathy, trust, confidence and joy, along with the ability to nurture ourselves and others, are now part of our being but when we were children were modeled by those around us. We internalized these developmental mileposts through the love, attention, limits and constancy of our early caretakers.

It is also through commitment and constancy that our adult relationships flourish. Hanging in there even through difficult times, whether it is in relationship to another human being or the artist's relationship with his or her art, constancy is the ultimate test of caring, love and devotion.

It is impossible to believe that our fast-moving world will ever be static. Change is inevitable, but the ability to accept change successfully occurs only when there is a foundation of constancy in our lives and relationships. Through research conducted in the early 1980s, Stinnett and DeFrain identified six characteristics of strong families. Commitment, time spent together and constancy were among the most important characteristics that strengthened the emotional well-being of family members. Eating dinner together, a weekly family night, love notes tucked inside your partner's briefcase, regular date nights with your beloved, recognition celebrations and so on are simple rituals that provide constancy. Constancy, in turn, strengthens adult relationships and helps form a solid foundation for children's lives. Closeness and trust are built on the constancy of shared experiences and routine reassurances found in everyday life. "No matter how much is going on outside of oneself, one still reaffirms what is on one's heart, taking comfort in the regular pulse. What works in the shelter of home or temple works everywhere. Only when we know such constancy will we know that our quest is succeeding" (Deng Ming-Dao).

"Tutu" Marjorie Valier

Love is something like the clouds that were in the sky before the sun came out. You can not touch the clouds, but you feel the rain and know how glad the flowers and the thirsty earth are to have it after a hot day. You cannot touch love either, but you feel the sweetness that it pours into everything.

—Annie Sullivan

Marjorie jumped from the pier in front of her house into the beautiful Pacific Ocean. At sixty, her lean, five-feet-nine-inch body was muscular, healthy and strong. She still swam two miles a day. As she walked back up to her house after her swim, she thought of how much she loved Hawaii: the beautiful ocean, the flowers, the gentle breeze against her cheek and her two beautiful grandchildren who would be with her tomorrow. She loved her grandchildren unconditionally, wanted what was best for them and hated the turmoil in their lives since their parents' divorce. She wanted to provide a sense of constancy and continuity in their lives, even if it was just during the twenty-four hours a month their father would allow her to have them.

The story of Marjorie Valier is based on an interview with her granddaughter, Sarah Healy. Sarah lives in Utah with her fiancé, Forrest, where she finds bliss working in her garden and hiking in the mountains. She grew up in Hawaii where her love for the ocean was born. One of her favorite memories is swimming in the ocean with her Tutu just off of the pier outside her home. Although her Tutu is no longer alive, Sarah carries her spirit with her and honors it every time she swims in the oceans of Hawaii.

Years later, Marjorie's now eighteen-year-old granddaughter, Sarah, swam to the same pier in front of the home her tutu (Hawaiian for "Grandmother") had left the year before, when she moved back to California. "When she moved, it was like losing my home," Sarah thought, treading water in front of the pier. She wanted just one more glimpse of the house that had been such a safe harbor during some of the roughest years of her life. This house meant many things to her: safety, peace, serenity, love, constancy, home. "The first time I had ever seen my mother sober was walking out of the door of that house only a few years ago," Sarah remembered. Then she turned and swam to the point farther down the beach where she had entered the water.

Sarah's parents had separated when she was four years old. Her mother moved from Hawaii to California. Sarah and her brother lived with their father and stepmother in Hawaii. They saw their mother only two or three times a year and were not allowed to refer to her or speak about her at home. The conflict and tension between family members was enormous and only increased from year to year.

"My tutu provided us with constancy, safety and the protection of the mother role," Sarah said. "She was adamant about maintaining contact with us and fought with my father to ensure that contact after he remarried. She was stubborn, unwilling to lose touch with us even if she had to go head-to-head with my father and stepmother, which she did many times. Yet she never brought that tension into our lives. She fought for as much time as she could have, but she had only twenty-four hours a month. Sadly for us, my father really regulated that time.

"She would pick us up after our crazy, tension-filled days and take us to her safe place. It was like a safe harbor, my secret garden, where there was serenity, peace, love and constancy. When my brother and

I got to Tutu's house, the three of us would just stand together for a few minutes on the lanai looking at the beautiful lawn with all the flowers, the hammock between the trees and out into the ocean, and I would know I was home. I was safe. No tension for twenty-four hours.

"There were regular rituals that I will never forget. We never watched television or movies. We received her full attention every minute of those twenty-four hours. She sat with us and read to us every night. I would lie on my belly with my shirt off while she gently rubbed and tickled my back with the tips of her fingers until I fell asleep. In the mornings we would take trays laden with guava juice and papayas, limes and other fruits, and we'd sit on the patio overlooking the ocean. The three of us ate together and talked. Many evenings we'd cut a milk carton in half, put a candle in it and set it off the pier into the ocean; then the three of us would sit for hours and watch it as it traveled across the waves until we couldn't see the light anymore. She'd always buy us Icees on the way home from the store. I would sit at her vanity table in her bedroom for hours putting on her makeup and trying on her jewelry. We'd talk and go for walks on the beach and sometimes go to art museums. These rituals may seem small, but they were enormous to me. They were my safety, and I built a life on them.

"My tutu was also my connection to my mother. We could talk about her and cry. She'd let us feel, and there were a lot of tears. She was never afraid of our emotions."

When Marjorie was in her late seventies, she moved back to California to live in the house her mother had willed to her. Even though her grandchildren were young adults, they felt they had lost their "home." Their tutu was their constant.

"At the end of her life, Tutu was still my teacher. She taught me about death. When she moved to California, her health began to decline. At seventy-five, she was still hiking eight miles with us, yet the loss of her beloved Hawaii was like losing her soul. She went back to Hawaii to die. At the end, she was surrounded by all she loved. My aunt and a friend would carry her into the water so she could feel the ocean on her skin. There was a gentle breeze in her room, and she was surrounded by the flowers of her beloved island.

"I was holding her hand when she took her last breath. That night I woke up at two in the morning; I didn't know why. I went into the room where my mother was sitting with my grandmother. I sat with Tutu so that my mother could get some sleep. I talked to my grandmother until the sun came up about my thankfulness for all she had given me, all the memories of the times with her that I treasured. I somehow knew she, like always, was listening to every word I said.

"Family tension increased at this time of impending loss, yet I didn't feel the tension while sitting with my tutu. I felt safe and serene like I had all the years of my childhood. I got to see the sun come up on her last day, and there was a beautiful breeze surrounding her. That last day and the days following her death, walking on the beach in Hawaii felt like grace. I felt in her death as I had in her life: safe, loved, protected and serene. She was the constancy in my life, my safe harbor even in her death."

Intentionally Bringing Constancy Back into Your Life

To have a true friendship, you have to do more than exchange Christmas cards or call each other once a year. There has to be some continued support and attention; otherwise the relationship is a sentimental attachment rather than a true friendship.

—DR. DOLORES KREISMAN

Intentionally Strengthen Friendships

- Make a list of the friendships you have considered important throughout your life. Have you let some go because of conflicts that you didn't have the energy to attempt to resolve? Did ties with important friends break through lack of care and feeding? Decide which friendships are important enough for you to nurture, and contact these friends at least once a week throughout the next year: cards, phone calls, visits and so on. If there is unresolved conflict, make a time with that friend to attempt to work it out. Let him or her know how important their friendship was to you.

Nurture Your Significant Other

- Sometimes we are too careless with those who mean the most to us. Healthy relationships have peaks and valleys. Contrary to those country-and-western love songs, in order to build trust, there must be times of conflict. Our ability to successfully resolve those conflicts is sometimes dependent on the good memories and appreciation stored in our "relationship savings accounts." Have a weekly date with your beloved (the same time every week is a good idea). Keeping this commitment takes work. Even if you are in different cities, there is always the telephone. Also, part of our savings account needs to be filled with appreciation. Often we find the time to criticize but not to appreciate. Discipline yourself to write a note of appreciation every week to your significant other.

Strengthen Constancy in Your Family

- One of the best ways to strengthen constancy in our families is through ritual. Ritual is any repeated, shared activity that has meaning for all members of the family—things they can depend on no matter what. Rituals provide what Sarah called her "safe harbor" during difficult times. Begin rituals in your family that young and old alike can depend on: Sunday dinner, game night, recognition nights, a week of camping every summer, regular special time with Grandma and so on.

Value THREE

Respect

To respect a person is not possible without knowing him; care and responsibility would be blind if they were not guided by knowledge.

—Erich Fromm

I was trying to decide which batteries I wanted for my tape recorder: the cheaper AAs or the ones with the slyly grinning bunny that were guaranteed to last longer. Suddenly, a child who appeared to be about six almost knocked me over. He held a plastic bag in his hand and was running from his harried mother, who soon came around the corner after him. "Put that back! Put it back, or there won't be any cookies!" she yelled. The boy just looked at her, holding a package of toy soldiers away from her as she tried to tackle him and confiscate the item. "Stop! Did you hear me?" The child obviously didn't, as they continued to wrestle for the toy soldiers his mother had said they could not buy.

A few minutes later, I was ahead of this dynamic duo at the checkout stand. The toy soldiers were lying on top of some chocolate-covered marshmallow cookies in the cart.

While standing in line, the little boy began grabbing for the candy on the shelves beside us. After she managed to wrestle away the candy, he grabbed a package of disposable razors. The boy thought this was great fun. The mother didn't. "Put that away or you won't have a birthday party next week," she threatened. "I mean it!"

The mother looked at me and the woman checking us out, obviously embarrassed. "Maybe those beltings my parents gave me weren't such a bad idea," she said with a sheepish smile. At least there was respect in those days." Then she said awkwardly, "Don't worry, I may want to belt him, but I won't. My husband and I decided we'd never raise our kids that way. We talk things out instead. He's just tired."

Later that evening I thought about this struggle between mother and child and about the hundreds of adults who had told me over the years, "There's just not any respect anymore!" The mother in the grocery store who had been "belted" by her parents probably was raised with fear and obedience, not respect. Later, when she tried to raise her own children in a better way, she knew not to "belt" them or teach them to fear her, but she seemed to have little idea how to set realistic limits, thereby gaining their respect for her, others and, ultimately, themselves.

When I asked the adults whom I interviewed in this book, "How did your grandmother discipline you?" without exception, there was silence, then, "I don't know that she had to punish me. Maybe she took away privileges or special things sometimes. I don't know. I just loved and respected her so much that I didn't want her to be disappointed in me." The other common attribute with all the grandmothers in this book is that they modeled values, listened, validated their grandchildren's feelings and needs, spent time with them, believed in their choices and capabilities, trusted them and expected them to do the right thing. In other words, they *respected* them. The grandchildren also witnessed their grandparents respecting others, nature, living things and themselves.

Fear should not be confused with respect. When someone says, "Respect me or else . . ." an individual may comply out of fear. Fear is "to be afraid of someone because they have power," whereas respect is to "admire someone because of his/her knowledge, skills, behavior and to be careful not to do anything against a person's rights or beliefs" (Longman, 2002). Fear is lethal, respect is nurturing. Fear is life threatening, whereas respect is life affirming. When one complies out of fear, the locus of control is external. When one complies out of respect, the impetus is internal.

True respect is not demanded, forced or bought. Employees may show respect for their bosses when in fact they fear them. Workers are much more likely to be more productive when employers have earned their respect. A religious leader can be either feared or respected. Nations or governments might be feared but not respected. People who are respected usually gain the voluntary cooperation of others without force or power. The difficulty with fear, as opposed to respect, is that when the powerful person or authority is no longer feared, the power base disappears and the person is left powerless, alone, unsupported, retaliated against or shunned.

People are more likely to respect the rights, beliefs and feelings of others and to honor and respect all living things when they first respect themselves, their beliefs, responsibilities and values. Respect and self-respect are deeply connected. It is impossible to respect others if we don't respect ourselves.

"Grandma Ginny" Mary Jane Thomas

There is no respect without humility in one's self.

—Henri Frederic Amriel

Eight-year-old Jan woke to the sound of her grandmother's voice calling her. Her grandmother was not in the room with her, but she could hear her voice just the same. She got up, got dressed and set off down the road to her grandmother's house. When she let herself into the house, she saw her grandmother by the stove, burning sacred tobacco and praying. When she was finished, she looked up at her granddaughter and said, "I'm glad you got my message. Today's the day you're old enough. There is something I want you to do."

There was a pond in the back of the house with a place cleared around it that resembled a well-cared-for country park. Her grandmother told Jan to sit by the pond, listen and pay attention to everything she saw, heard and experienced, and everything told to her. Later Jan came back from the pond, and her grandmother asked her what she had seen and heard. "I didn't see anything," Jan replied, so her grandmother told her to go back again. This happened two

The story of Mary Jane Thomas is based on an interview with her granddaughter Jan Longboat. Jan made a decision years ago to dedicate herself to the medicines. "If we nurture our own gifts, the Creator will truly look after us." Jan is currently the keeper of "Earth Healing Herb Gardens" on Six Nations of the Grand River.

more times with little Jan returning each time and sadly reporting that she hadn't seen anything. By the third time, Jan was starting to feel anxious.

On the fourth trip to the pond, Jan saw her reflection in the water. All of a sudden her senses kicked in, and she could smell the land around her as she never had before. She could see the medicines and the trees. She could hear the birds singing and all the flying insects buzzing around her. She could feel the cool breeze on her face and her arms. Jan was frightened of her heightened senses and ran into the house to tell her grandmother what she had experienced. Her grandmother told her that this was what she wanted her to see and feel and that now she was old enough to help with the medicines. She said that if she could not see and hear clearly she couldn't work with the medicines, because when they spoke to her she would not be able to hear them.

"That was the first time I truly saw me," Jan said. "It wasn't until I was an adult that I realized all of the lessons my grandmother taught me that day: respect for myself and all of creation. I began to know myself for the first time. She said to me, 'Now you know these gifts to you from Shonkwaia'tison (the Creator), five plus two: seeing, smelling, hearing, touching, tasting and two more gifts that will take you through life. One will take you down the roughest road, and you'll never fall down; the other will get you through the darkest night, and you'll never get lost.' She was talking about the gifts of intuition and telepathy: the powers of the mind. 'Your gifts from Shonkwaia'tison are five plus two,' she said."

Mary Jane Thomas never cut her hair. She put it in a bun or braided it around her head. She built her own house and lived off the land. She was a gardener and grew fruits, vegetables and medicines to share with everyone. She had lots of fruit trees, wild blueberries and raspberries. She spoke four languages: Onondaga, Mohawk, Cayuga and a little bit of Tuscarora. She didn't have electricity, running water or a well, just a six foot hole that never went dry. She was a strong woman who respected herself and all life. She was also a visionary.

People came to her from all over. She never locked her door, always had water heating on the stove and a light turned low on her table. She wanted to help people stay well. "People would come with lanterns down the path to her house," Jan said. "They would talk and she would listen, then she'd get medicines from the baskets hanging on the logs across the ceiling and give it to them. When she picked the medicines, she would always put down the sacred tobacco that she carried in a handkerchief pinned inside her dress, close to her heart, and thank the Creator for these gifts from the earth. Her medicines would make people well. They in turn would bring her potatoes, chickens or a jar of fruit. She opened her door to all people, and now that's also how I live."

Grandma Ginny could sit for hours and just be quiet. She had inner peace and never was afraid. "She taught us to respect all life and to get up early in the morning, watch the sun come up and thank the earth for everything we were given. We learned from her how to respect the cycles of life and not to let time pass unnoticed: time to plant, to harvest, to pick the roots or the bark, or to wash our faces in the dew. She taught us to honor the earth, the universe, all that lives, always letting it teach us.

"She taught her granddaughters the powers and responsibilities given to women: to look after the earth, the land, the medicines, the children and to give life. She taught me to see, to touch, to feel and to listen to everything around me and inside me, to respect myself and the gifts that I was given."

Jan was living away from home when her grandmother became ill, and just like that morning when she was eight years old, Grandma Ginny called her home. Jan listened to that voice inside her, as she was taught, and came home. Her grandmother was eighty years old and had never been sick nor seen a doctor in her life. "When she saw me, she said, 'Good, you got my message.' I drove her to a doctor. That was the day she died. Even in death she gave me strength, because she always taught me to respect death as a natural part of the cycle of life."

Strengthening Respect for Ourselves, Others and All Living Things

Self-respect is not a matter of what you are doing in your life, but rather of how you are doing it. It requires that you bring quality and virtue into each action, whatever that action may be.

—Dadi Janki

Self-Respect

- In the Respect section of your "Values Journal," write all of the ways you show respect for yourself and all of the ways that you don't. Include goals for increasing your self-respect. (For example, I respect myself when I don't allow others to shame me but, instead, let them know what I feel and need. I do not respect myself when I allow others to put me down or I put myself down. I will ask people to stop if they are shaming me or I will pay attention to the shaming I give myself.)

Respect for Others

- Make five columns in the Respect section of your journal. In the first column, list all of those people in your life today: your partner, children, co-workers, boss, friends, minister, mother and father, for example. In the second column, write any fears you have in relation to them. (A wife may write: I fear that my husband will leave me if I state my opinions.) In the third column, write all the ways you truly respect them. (I respect my husband's ability to make decisions, his work, the way he takes care of himself.) In the fourth column, write how your fear is affecting your behavior. (I am silent, or I agree with his opinion, or I disrespect myself.) Sometimes our fears cause us to do things that disrespect ourselves—

keep silent, promise things we won't do—or disrespect others—yell, threaten, withhold. Be honest with yourself. In the last column, write ways in which you can empower yourself to change the relationship.

Respect for All Living Things

- Make three columns in the Respect section of your journal. In one column, write your values regarding other people and all living things. (For instance, I believe in helping and being respectful to the elderly. I honor the beliefs and values of people from different cultures. I believe in taking care of our environment.) In the second column, write the ways you have disrespected your own values. (For example, an elderly woman was behind me in the grocery store, and I was in too much of a rush to let her go before me. Or, I know my aunt is out of wood, but I haven't offered to cut some for her.) In the third column, write ways in which you will be more respectful and committed to your values.

Hard Work

He that would eat the fruit
must climb the tree.

—James Kelly

Four years ago, my son and I were shopping for a bed for his new apartment. The store was huge, confusing—a literal warehouse of choices. After a lengthy period of feeling overwhelmed, we finally found the perfect bed in one of the many displays throughout the store. How to actually purchase the bed was a mystery. Thus began a lengthy search for an employee to answer our questions and help us order the bed. Where were the salespeople? We found no one to help us. Finally, at the end of a long aisle was another display featuring an entire bedroom set. Sitting, leaning and lying on the bed were six employees talking and laughing. I was flabbergasted. I turned to my son and started one of those judgmental statements the older generation makes that, in my younger days, I swore I never would, "What has happened to pride in hard work? In my day . . ." I caught myself, realizing that going down this particular path was not going to help.

My attitude in check, I walked over to the group. After an uncomfortable period waiting for one of them to finish an interminable story, I said, "Excuse me." I had to say this several times because one of them was beginning yet another story. I raised my voice an octave, "Could someone please help us? We want to buy a bed." Now that I had their attention, six faces looked up at me seemingly annoyed by my interruption. One replied, "I will be with you in a minute," and returned to the story. Now I was speechless.

On the January 24, 2005, cover of *Time* magazine, a young adult is sitting in a sandbox. To the left of this picture is the statement, "They're not lazy, they just won't grow up." Lev Grossman calls them the "twixters," a generation of people who are not kids anymore but not adults either. "Who are these permanent adolescents, these twenty-something Peter Pans? And why can't they grow up? Everybody knows a few—full grown men and women who still live with their parents, who dress and talk and party as they did in their teens, hopping from job to job and from date to date, having fun but seemingly going nowhere. . . . This isn't just a trend, a temporary fad or a generational hiccup. This is a much larger phenomenon of a different kind and a different order" (Grossman, 2005, 42).

Reasons for this change in diligence and pride in hard work are varied according to a variety of experts: mass divorces in previous generations, the breakdown of the extended family, a belief in the dishonesty and lack of loyalty from the corporations we work for, being raised with "me" values rather than "we" values, a lack of mentoring, financial needs being taken care of by mom and dad, perceived unhappiness in the adult population, a shift in the economic foundation that used to support adolescents on their way to adulthood (young adults who can't afford to grow up financially), a belief that nothing lasts, children raised with values of immediate gratification and focus on "being happy" and "self-actualized" rather than "diligence" and "responsibility."

Taking pride in hard work well done has as its core self-esteem, value and purpose. Pride and joy in hard work is a learning process. Many people have gone much further and accomplished more than they ever thought possible because someone believed in them and expected the best from them. Others have never lived up to their capabilities. They have difficulty feeling pride in their work, in part because people have shown that they don't believe in them or what they could accomplish by (1) continually criticizing them, (2) consistently expecting less than what they could accomplish, (3) expecting more than what they could reasonably accomplish and/or (4) expecting results without their ever having been taught or mentored. Individuals' lack of pride in hard work well done may be the result of early teachings by role models that it is acceptable to make excuses when tasks are not completed satisfactorily. Or they may have developed a sense of entitlement by being given unearned positions, money or possessions.

When we are expected to give our best, view our mistakes and setbacks as teachers, and take pride in hard work accomplished, we develop courage, determination and self-worth.

Grandma "Gertie"
Lola Gertrude Harrmann

Children are likely to live up to
what you believe of them.

—Lady Bird Johnson

The corn had been harvested and the shellers had come and gone. On top of the twenty-foot-high pile of corncobs, her dress hitched between her legs, sixty-five-year-old Grandma Gertie, laughing with abandon, slid down the pile, closely followed by her grandchildren. She always believed in and modeled working hard and having fun.

"Grandma would talk to us about the importance of hard work and was also one of the most fun-loving people I have ever known," her grandson, Terry, recalled. "We would have worked hard for a couple of hours picking strawberries when all of a sudden, *splat,* an overripe strawberry would hit me on the cheek. I'd look up from my work and see the twinkle in my grandmother's eyes, and I would know that it was time for fun to begin."

Gertrude Harrmann, Gertie, was a small woman, five feet one and always skinny. She lived on a farm all of her life. When she was young, she rode her horse to school. At age ten or eleven, she would ride over on her lunch hour to the hotel where her mother worked as a cook, make pies and then ride back to school. After school,

---

The story of Lola Gertrude Harrmann is based on an interview with her grandson, Terry Harrmann. "Grandmother's gentle hand is still felt by me and also the great-grandchildren that, because of her long life, got to know her. We learned the importance of integrity, honesty, hard work, and a never-ending sense of humor."

she'd go home and do all of her chores. She worked hard all of her life. "My grandmother would always tell us that there's no shame in having dirt or flour under your fingernails," Terry said. "Any kind of work was honorable, and if you did the best work you could, it didn't matter what kind of a job it was, you were fulfilling what you were supposed to be doing."

Gertie raised her family with hard work, love and play. She did all the chores first thing in the morning and then made breakfast for all the "thrashers" who came to thrash the oats. The family raised corn, soybeans and oats. She cooked all day to feed everyone lunch and dinner, and she made her own butter, jam and bread. They grew all their own food on their farm. They used what they needed from what they grew and produced on the farm: fruits and vegetables, grains, milk, eggs and meat and sold the rest. When Terry's father began his own family, he still farmed with his parents. He and his new family lived in a small house right up the road. "We didn't have much money; we worked hard and were rich in love. It didn't matter how old she was, my grandmother always mixed work and fun. She was amazing: she milked the cows morning and night and did all this work, but always took time to play with us. I remember walking up to her house from the time I was little until I was a grown man. I'd walk past the window, and she'd throw water out the screen. A water fight would begin. The next day, I'd always get her back. Gertie was always fun, loved to play, but also could set boundaries when our behavior got out of line.

"She would let us play with anything in her house. She wouldn't tell us "no" or yell at us. She trusted us to be responsible, and she never lectured. She'd tell us, 'I'd really be disappointed if you guys did (whatever).' I would have rather cut off my arm than let my grandmother down.

"I was driving into town to the feed mill when I was thirteen or fourteen. I was underage to drive a car but everyone in farm country did it. My parents would give me the checkbook to pick up feed. That's the kind of trust and responsibility I was given. I did the same thing with my own kids, and they never let me down. It seems like many adults today don't expect hard work, responsibility or trust from youth, and they get what they expect."

Gertie always told her grandchildren they could do anything they set their minds to and could make their dreams come true if they worked hard and were disciplined enough to save even a little money every day. "She always told us to put away a nickel or a dime every day. She'd say, 'Drop it in the can, and let it go,'" Terry said, smiling at the memory, "When she was around eighty, before my grandparents moved into a house in town, she took us to the basement of the farmhouse and directed us to the fruit cellar. In a special hiding place was a big lard tin. She told us to go get the can. It was so heavy because it was filled to the brim with the money she had saved a nickel and dime at a time throughout her life. When they moved off the farm into town, they had saved enough to pay cash for their house."

Terry's friends loved coming to his grandparents' farm to help with the work just to have the opportunity to talk to Grandma Gertie. They talked to her about anything that was troubling them and always valued what she had to say. "We never had problems getting kids from town to come out and help us bale hay or any other chore because they loved my grandmother," Terry said proudly. "It was amazing seeing her talking and playing with all my high school friends. She was the unofficial "counselor" for so many people, young or old, in our town, and she never had finished high school, let alone college."

Terry's father had a heart attack when Gertie was in her nineties. He was too ill to look after her. Terry's grandfather and mother had already died, and Terry and his sister had moved away, so Gertie had to spend her remaining days in a nursing home. "She died in my arms three weeks before she turned 101," Terry said with tears in his eyes. "I told her it was all right to just let go. At the funeral, nursing home staff that had come and gone during the years were there. Even eighteen-year-olds working at the home shortly before her death told me that they had talked with her often about their problems: money, relationships, work, and so on. She had counseled all of them and gave them good advice. She made community and family no matter where she went."

Grandma Gertie always brought homemade lemonade and store-bought lemon cookies to Terry when he was hard at work in the field. His children knew the special place to find the lemon cookies in her home, and there was always a pitcher of lemonade in the refrigerator. "Even when she was in the nursing home and the house was empty, she would instruct my father to always keep lemonade in the refrigerator and lemon cookies in the special cupboard for her great-grandchildren. When my grandmother died, my girls were in high school. We went to the house, and the cookies were still there.

"I was busy and ambitious, and it was important to Grandma that I spend lots of time with my children. Even as old as she was, my children always wanted to go to Grandma Gertie's. There had always been hard work, play, love and special things, like those lemon cookies, that grounded us. Our parents and grandparents—the center of our home—were our role models and mentors who expected responsibility, trust and our best efforts. Their teachings remain inside of us, generation upon generation."

Developing Pride and Joy in Work Well Done

No one can arrive from being talented alone.
God gives talent, work transforms talent into genius.

—Anna Pavlova

Life Mentors: Who Were They and What Did They Teach?

- In the Hard Work section of your "Values Journal," list role models you had early in life who taught you about work: parents, grandparents, extended family, and so on. List what you learned from each person and how that teaching is affecting your life today. What changes would you like to make and why? (For example, my mother would always yell at me to do chores around the house. When I didn't do them, which was most of the time, she would do them, and then I would feel guilty. I learned that people would do things for me. I have fights with my wife all the time about what I do or don't do around the house. She yells too but continues to do the majority of the work. I never realized this pattern before. The more she does, the less I do.)
- Now list the mentors you have had in your life: teachers, community members, coaches and so on. What did you learn from each of them? Did you feel trusted, respected and valued, as Terry did with his grandmother? How has that mentor affected your life? If you have never had a mentor, think of a task that you want to learn (woodworking, quilting, sailing), and find a mentor who is willing to teach you.
- Have you ever been a mentor? Did your approach foster confidence, self-respect and pride in a job well done? If you have never been a mentor or have not mentored for a long time, think of a skill that you are willing to share with a young person. Go to your local school or boys or girls club and offer to mentor a young person.

Evaluate Your Work and Career Choices

- Are you satisfied with the way you approach your work (work in general)? Do you feel pride in what you do? Do you work for an organization that values their employees or do you feel devalued? How do the climate, loyalty and responsibility of your workplace affect how you do your job? Are your efforts noticed and praised or are your mistakes the only things that are noticed? Do you complete tasks or do you leave them half-finished? Do you blame others when tasks are not completed well or on time? Are there changes you would like to make? How will you approach making the changes?

Obtain Balance in Work and Play

- Make a circle in the Hard Work section of your "Values Journal." Think of all the things you spend time doing every week: work, time alone, significant other, family, children, friends, play, spirituality, self-care, rest, TV and anything else you normally do. Use a seventeen- or eighteen-hour day as a guide (twenty-four hours minus seven or eight hours for sleep times seven). The time each week should be approximately 119 hours. List the amount of time spent this week on each area. (For instance, forty hours work, fourteen hours play, ten hours time with my significant other, fifty hours with family, fourteen hours with my children or grandchildren, seven hours alone, and so on.) Assign an appropriate amount of space in the circle for the time you spent in each area. Is your life in balance? If not, set some goals for putting your life back in balance. List your goals and how you want to reassign areas of your life. The following week, reevaluate how you've done.

Value FIVE

Compassion

If someone listens, or stretches out a hand,
or whispers a kind word of encouragement, or
attempts to understand a lonely person,
extraordinary things begin to happen.

—Loretta Girzartis

A chubby little hand tightly grasping four beautiful flowers appears in the line of sight of a young mother crying in frustration. Her child, in an effort to soothe her, has spent time carefully selecting each flower for this offering. Will the mother ignore the child's gift of compassion, push the child away, yell at the child for picking her flowers, or bring her child close in a big bear hug, appreciating the depths of empathy and compassion in this kind gesture?

Compassion is the concern we feel for the welfare of others. It is understanding and caring for those who are hurting, allowing our love to touch the pain of another. It is a desire to help, to alleviate the suffering of another, even if the only help we can offer is a kind word or gesture or to stand with the other when he or she is in pain. Compassion is not pity. Pity is rooted in fear that is cloaked in arrogance and often disdain. Nor is compassion the need to please or "fix" others in order to compensate for our shattered self-esteem. When we are compassionate, our love touches the pain of others. In order to feel compassion for others, we must first feel compassion for ourselves.

"In discussing compassion, the Tibetan word *Tse-wa,* there is also a sense to the word of its being a state of mind that can include a wish for good things for oneself. In developing compassion, perhaps one could begin with the wish that oneself be free of suffering, and then take that natural feeling towards oneself and cultivate it, enhance it, and extend it out to include and embrace others" (Dalai Lama, 1998, 114).

Research shows that "compassion is deeply rooted in our brains, our bodies, and in the most basic ways we communicate. What's more, a sense of compassion fosters compassionate behavior and helps shape the lessons we teach our children" (Keltner, 2004). Compassion, which role models show for themselves, children, others and all living things, nurtures the tools of compassion in children and is the cornerstone for their well-being and their sense of purpose in life.

"Nonee"
Hazel Inez Jules Salle

She did not talk to people as if they were
strange hard shells she had to crack open to get inside.
She talked as if she were already in the shell.
In their very shell.

—Marita Bonner

Carlie's laughter and obvious joy of life could lighten up a room. I realized as I watched her offer support to a sobbing woman, who had been relating a story of a painful experience in her life, that Carlie's love and compassion seemed to touch the very core of the woman's being.

I knew that Carlie had painful experiences in her young life, and I asked her where the joy and compassion she radiated came from. She smiled, literally glowing from the inside out, "My Nonee. My wonderful Nonee."

"My Nonee was all about doing whatever would make you happy and fill you with joy. She called me her 'comfy, cozy sweetheart,' and she always taught me to trust my inner feelings. She'd always tell me to trust myself, to know what I wanted and go for it. She would say, 'My granddaughter, she knows what she likes and what she needs.'"

The story of Hazel Inez Jules Salle is based on an interview with her granddaughter, Carlie Chase. Carlie is twenty-seven years old and is from the Shuswap Nation in British Columbia. She is the daughter of Karen Chase, Inez's daughter. Carlie graduated from the University of British Columbia and works in the Aboriginal health field. She is actively involved in the Canadian Institute for Conflict Resolution and the City for All Women Initiative in Ottawa. She has recently developed a passion for hand drumming. "The compassionate spirit of my grandmother walks with me every day of my life."

Carlie described her younger life in her family as one of "walking on eggshells." She said her mother was wonderful, but the family lived in the shadow of her father's severe emotional abuse and his physical abuse of their mother. "He was a 'rageaholic.' I was never smart enough, fast enough, good enough. But when my brother and I would go to my grandparents', they would bring joy back into our lives. Nonee would always tell me, 'Don't you worry, sweetheart, just keep on doing what you're doing and being the beautiful person you are. You're doing just fine.'"

Hazel Inez Salle was First Nations. She was Shuswap from British Columbia. She, like thousands of First Nations children, had been taken from her family and put into a residential school, where she lived from age five to seventeen. "She learned in the residential school that she was a 'dirty Indian' and not as good as others," Carlie said sadly. "But through all that shame, she retained her love and compassion. She loved her daughter and grandchildren unconditionally. She was the matriarch and wisdom keeper of our family. Nonee was loving, firm and strong. When we did something we weren't supposed to, she would respond immediately. She had a look that told us we were doing something other than what she expected; then she would change the subject or switch the focus, and we learned quickly not to do it again. She never yelled or punished.

"She taught me love and compassion for myself and also for others. She was so kind to everyone. One summer she had a friend who came drunk to her house. She was so kind and compassionate to the man. I'd never seen a drunken person, and I got really scared and started to cry. She gently took me into her bedroom and comforted me. She never said an unkind word about the man. She just held me and rocked me. She said, 'Oh, sweetheart, it's just growing pains, just growing pains.' Now whenever I am in grief, I hear her words and feel comfort inside me."

Inez showed Carlie unconditional love. She supported Carlie's own special way of relating to the world and helped her be the compassionate person she is today. Even though she lived two hours away, Inez was always there to share in every joy, every disappointment, every holiday, birthday and event that was important to young Carlie. "When I was around seven, I had a soccer game in a town a ways from home. I called my grandparents and said, 'Come to my game. I'm taking this game on the road.' They dropped everything and came.

"When we'd go to my grandparents' house, they would see the car coming down the road and we waved and were happy. I'd see Nonee on the porch and begin to relax. It was like the tension would flow out of my young body the minute I saw her. She would give me a big hug and rock me back and forth saying again and again, 'I'm so glad you're here, sweetheart.' We'd walk into the house and see pictures of ourselves everywhere. There would always be special treats waiting for us on the coffee table.

"She was a plump woman with thick, black hair and beautiful skin, not a wrinkle. She loved to wear vibrant colors: purples, greens and reds. She had fabulous turquoise jewelry, and I'll always remember her perfectly sculpted long, lean, graceful and gentle hands."

To Carlie, Nonee's house was a peaceful, relaxed haven. They'd take long walks on summer evenings, and Carlie would jump into bed with her grandparents in the morning. She would help Nonee cook and make bread and help her in the garden. "She had the most beautiful, amazing garden; vegetables, flowers, beautiful rose bushes. It was lovingly cared for like everything else in Nonee's life," Carlie said proudly.

"She would save all these little Avon lipsticks for me. I'd put on the lipstick and really make a mess of her spotless bathroom when I was little. That was fine with her. She would always leave some of my little fingerprints on the wall. Her house was always immaculate, and when my mother would come to pick us up she'd tell Nonee that there were little red fingerprints on her bathroom wall. Nonee would say, 'Those are from my granddaughter's little fingers, and I'm going to keep them there.'

"She saved absolutely everything of my brother's and mine. She had boxes of all our letters, drawings and even our scribbles. When she was in the hospital in the last months of her life, she asked me to bring her the box. She wanted me to read her some of the letters that my brother and I had written to her over the years.

"When I was an adult and had moved away, we still would talk on the phone once or twice a week. She would always end the phone conversation with, 'I'll love you forever, sweetheart.' And when she was with me, as old as I was, she'd hug me and rock me and say, 'I will love you for ever and ever.'

"When she was dying, I'd lie in her hospital bed with her, and when we were alone I'd hold her and cry and tell her, 'I'll love you for ever and ever and ever.'

"I brought all of my Nonee's unconditional love, compassion and joy inside me. I have the compassion and joy that I have because she fought for me. I have so much of her inside me. As loving as she was, I think she literally changed my DNA, every cell to the core of my being. I miss her, yet the close connection we shared is not bound by the physical world. I feel her spirit with me every day of my life."

Living a Life of Compassion

We who lived in concentration camps can
remember the men who walked through the huts
comforting others, giving away their last piece of bread.
They may have been few in number, but they offer sufficient
proof that everything can be taken from a man but
one thing: the last of the human freedoms—to choose
one's attitude in any given set of circumstances,
to choose one's own way.

—Viktor Frankl

Show Compassion for Yourself

- Write the ways that you show compassion for yourself in the Compassion section of your "Values Journal." How do you take care of yourself physically, emotionally, spiritually and mentally? Are you gentle with yourself, or do you demand perfection? Do you place harsh judgments on yourself? Are you true to yourself and listen and trust your intuition? If you are unkind, harsh or critical of yourself, where does the criticism and unkindness come from? Give a name to the critical voice that has said these things to you in the past.
- Give a name to the supportive messages you give to yourself and identify sources of those positive affirmations. For instance, Carlie was kind to herself in much the same way Nonee was to her. Work to override criticism and unfair judgments you make of yourself. Instead, feed yourself messages of compassion. Hurtful message: You shouldn't make mistakes. Compassionate message: Mistakes are gifts. They teach me of my humanity and help me to learn.

Show Compassion for Others

- Pay attention to your thoughts and actions over the next week. Are there times when you find yourself being critical and/or making judgments about others? Are there times when you have talked about others unfairly or injured another with gossip or unkind words? Have you seen someone hurting and walked by him or her without helping? Examine your list at the end of the week. Find a quiet place, close your eyes and one at a time bring the person you have judged, hurt or ignored into focus. Imagine them sitting in front of you. Focus on what it would be like to be them. Are you critical or judgmental because you disown or fear some of the qualities you see in them? Awareness is the first step to changing unhealthy behavior. Name it. Feel it. Own it. Change it.

Teach Children to Be Compassionate

- It is not just a cliché that "our children are our future." If we want a compassionate world, we must teach compassion to our children, grandchildren, nieces or nephews. Spend time with a child this week. Help the child complete an act of compassion. Here are some fun examples:

    1. Help the child go through his or her toys and select ones that are no longer used. Take them to a place that collects toys and distributes them to children who do not have them.
    2. Help the child with a garage sale or lemonade stand and give the money to a charitable organization. Many children helped those who were affected by the December 2004 tsunami or the 9/11 tragedy in just this way. It helped them process these tragedies.
    3. Take an older child with you when you volunteer to help others.

Kindness

One kind word can warm three winter months.

—Japanese Proverb

Barrey Saunders, staff writer for the *News and Observer* writes: "Instead of some weapon of mass destruction bringing about the world's end, it'll most likely be a weapon of indifference. . . ." A world without kindness will be our undoing.

Many psychologists have written about humankind's natural inclination toward aggressiveness. I believe that most of us lean toward helpfulness and kindness, yet sometimes our fears and feelings of helplessness lead us instead to express anger or indifference. Fears that our offerings of kindness will result in violence are often supported and encouraged by news reports that magnify the attacks on a few people who offer assistance to others. The belief that we have little to offer is fed by an overabundance of experts, specialties and lawsuits.

My belief in the inherent kindness of people is nurtured by the hundreds of individuals who offer assistance at times of natural or man-made disaster and the daily offerings of help to others by individuals who have no expectation of reward or fame. Thousands of people go the extra mile for others every day just because they're kind and caring human beings. If these kind and giving role models were highlighted in nightly news reports, it might serve to underscore the value of kindness rather than reinforce the growing trend toward indifference. These unsung heroes might offer hope and inspiration to a new generation of young people who want to help others but are afraid or feel unworthy to do so.

Many have told me that their natural inclination is to offer kindness but they feel unworthy because they are not "experts." Others see the world through lenses of fear that paralyze them and cause them to continually suspect the worst in others, which then triggers more fear. It becomes a self-fulfilling prophecy: learned helplessness and fear is fertile ground for indifference, depression and anger, and anger and isolation become a breeding ground for fear. This notion as is exemplified by an ancient proverb by Lao-tzu (604–531 BC):

> Once upon a time a man whose ax was missing suspected his neighbor's son. The boy walked like a thief, looked like a thief and spoke like a thief. But the man found his ax while digging in the valley, and the next time he saw his neighbor's son, the boy walked, looked and spoke like any other child.

"Bachan"
Itoe Kawamoto

Constant kindness can accomplish much.
As the sun makes ice melt, kindness causes
misunderstanding, mistrust and
hostility to evaporate.

—ALBERT SCHWEITZER

Young Rod was worried about Bachan (Japanese for "grandmother") as he walked down the street holding her hand. She was thin and small, four feet nine or ten, and spoke to "absolutely everyone." He felt protective of her as was traditional for a grandson in Japanese culture. It wasn't a good neighborhood; there were a lot of homeless people and gang members, and some of them frightened eight-year-old Rod. He was nervous for her because she thought everyone was "the nicest person."

In a matter of a block, she would warmly greet at least eight people, usually more. It didn't matter to her who they were; she said "hi" to them. Young Rod needn't have worried. His grandmother lived in the same neighborhood for years, and no one hurt her. She was kind, and what she gave out, she got back.

"It blew my mind," Rod said. "She'd say 'hi' to gang members, and you could see by the expressions on their faces that they couldn't understand why she was being so nice to them. Her

---

The story of Itoe Kawamoto is based on an interview with her grandson, Rod Kawamoto. Rod was born and raised in Richmond, British Columbia, Canada. "I live my life based on the values my Bachan taught me."

kindness shocked them. I didn't want her to speak to some of these people who seemed very frightening to me, but she did anyway. Through her kindness, they were also kind. I remember this homeless man sitting in front of a store. She leaned over and gave him a great big smile and said 'hi.' You could tell by his face that he was a bit stunned, but he soon smiled broadly and said 'hello' to her. She was the kindest person I have ever met, and she taught me the values of kindness and respect every day until the day she died."

Itoe Kawamoto was born in Japan in 1908 and lived there until her family immigrated to Canada when Itoe was eleven. She lived most of her life in Vancouver, British Columbia. During the Second World War, she, like many Japanese Canadians and Japanese Americans, was relocated. She was placed in East Vancouver where she lived until she died in 1992. Her husband died when Rod's father was twelve. Itoe was a maid for a family on the west end of Vancouver for forty-five years. She began working for them when she was twenty years old and retired at sixty-five. The family's children grew up with her, then had their own children who also employed Itoe. "In her later years," Rod said, "I think they kept Bachan on even though she couldn't do as much as she once had. They respected her and treated her well personally and financially."

She lived in an old-style ranch house that had a really big basement. This unfinished basement was the scene of many weekly hockey games and much joy for her eight grandchildren. A fridge was always stocked with each grandchild's favorite food and lots of ice cream. All eight of her grandchildren were at her house every Sunday.

"She would be very tired after work, but if she knew we were coming over, she would make homemade lemon tarts and bread, chow mien, sushi—all of our favorite foods. She'd sit us at the table and ask each of us what was going on in our lives. We could talk to her about anything, even with the language barrier (she understood some English and we understood some Japanese). I will always remember how much she communicated with her eyes and through her facial expressions. When we finished eating and talking, she'd give each of us a big hug."

"She always treated us equally," Rod said. "It didn't matter who had the best grades or who was best in sports. To Bachan we were all the same. She treated us all with love, respect and kindness. We were pressured in other places of our lives to do well, but with Bachan we felt safe, loved and accepted, and there was much laughter."

Itoe's house was filled with people from all walks of life; no matter who they were, she was always kind and respectful toward them, always offering food and waiting on them. She treated everyone exactly the same and was concerned about each person. She talked little about herself; instead she was interested in others.

"It was always about you, never about her," Rod said. "I remember there was a man whose wife died, and his family was still in Japan. Bachan fed him every day and treated the man as if he were a king. She took care to make a special feast for him, no matter how tired she was. His meals always included homemade chow mien and noodles. In later years, she had bad knees and arthritis but never complained about herself. Instead she would ask others how they were. She personified grace and humility."

It is traditional in Japanese culture for the grandchildren to take care of their grandparents when they age. Itoe thought her grandchildren should focus on their own lives for as long as possible, so even though Rod's parents built a house with a space in it for her, Itoe chose to live in her own house until she died at eighty-three.

Although the family always came to her house on Sundays, she would take the long bus ride to Rod's house many times a week to be with her children and grandchildren. She never let them drive her.

"Even when she was tired after working all day, she'd always make the long bus trip to bring us treats or come to our hockey games," Rod said. "She'd be in the stands, cheering us on, even though I knew she didn't understand hockey. When she'd get a bonus on Christmas, she shared it with all of us.

"The last time I saw Bachan, she had taken the long bus ride to visit us. She had a stroke in the kitchen and was taken to the hospital where she died shortly after being admitted, surrounded by the family who cherished her.

"On special occasions or when I have even the smallest success, I think of Bachan. Daily, I try to be like she was and emulate her kindness and humility. I look for the good in everyone, and although many people have commented that they really don't understand it, when I have anything, even a small piece of food, I share it just like she did. I am a happier person because I have learned to be kind. I now fully understand the joy it brought her to be kind to everyone because I often experience that joy. She taught me the value of kindness and self-respect; she taught it and lived it."

Acts of Kindness

There are two ways of spreading light:
to be the candle or the mirror that reflects it.

—Edith Wharton

Explore Your Fears

- This week be aware of the many times that you have the natural inclination to assist another but your fear stops you. Write these in the Kindness section of your "Values Journal." Fear, if it's warranted, can be a very helpful emotion. It warns us of danger. If unjustified, it can also produce needless anxiety, isolation and indifference. After each journal entry, explore whether the fear of offering kindness and assistance to another is grounded in reality. (For instance, a woman driving down the interstate sees a strange man thumbing a ride. Her fear of stopping and offering him a ride may be well founded. Now imagine her driving down the street and seeing someone that is a familiar face in her community standing by a broken down car and needing assistance. Fearfulness in this case may be unwarranted.) Examine your list at the end of the week and determine how many times you didn't offer help because of unsubstantiated fear or because you believed you weren't competent to help or that someone else would do it. Maybe you were in a hurry or you just "didn't want to get involved."

Strengthen Your Awareness of Kindness

- Be aware of acts of kindness around you this week. Look up "kindness" and "acts of kindness" on the Internet. Surround yourself with the kindness of others. At the end of the week, take a few minutes to relax, close your eyes and imagine a world where people assisted one another regularly, not merely in times of crises. How would it feel to live in such a world? What can be your part in helping this image become a reality?

Take the Time for Kindness

- Greet every person you pass with a smile and a warm "hello" as Bachan modeled so well. What are their reactions to your caring and kindness? Go out of your way to perform one act of kindness this week for a neighbor, work associate or fellow community member. Was your act of kindness accepted or were your efforts rejected? How did this offering of kindness make you feel?

Gratitude

Blessed are those that can give without remembering and receive without forgetting.

—Author Unknown

The seven-year-old boy with cotton candy in one hand and tickets for more rides in the other throws a full-blown tantrum because his grandmother won't give him money for a toy at the amusement park. A seventeen-year-old girl gives her parents the silent treatment for two days because they didn't have enough money to buy her the expensive prom dress she wanted. A corporate boss bullies his employees because they didn't top last year's sales or increase its considerable profit margin. What has happened to "gratitude"?

I often hear parents say, "I want my child to feel special, to be the center of my world. I don't want my child to feel guilty for wants and needs like I did." Yet these same parents are surprised when their children show little appreciation for what they are given and instead increasingly want more. Many children today are encouraged by adults and advertisements to believe they deserve everything they get and are entitled to everything they want. Often the more material things children receive without earning them, the less gratitude they show. These children don't feel a sense of guilt for demanding more; the parents feel guilt because they do not have the means to give more.

Over the years, the pendulum has swung from children feeling guilty for their needs and wants because they were to be "seen and not heard" and knew their parents had little to give in time or material things to where they feel entitled to anything they want and are angry if they don't get it. Unfortunately we have passed five and, as is often the case with change, are fast reaching ten.

It has become almost "petty" to want to be thanked for giving to or doing something for someone. Some people believe it is out of style to show appreciation or to say "please" and "thank you." Yet adults tell me they are hurt when they don't receive appreciation from their employers, friends or children for what they give or do. The foundation for gratitude and empathy (the ability to feel for another) is losing ground as we speed along the highway from "we" to "me."

Many people have voiced the belief that gratitude for the things we have could lead to complacency, yet research shows that grateful people reported more instances of positive emotions, greater life satisfaction, vitality and optimism, and fewer instances of depression and stress than their less grateful counterparts. These same grateful people also showed enhanced pleasurable feelings, diminished unpleasant emotions, less likelihood of judging their own success in terms of the accumulation of possessions and were more likely to share their possessions with others. Grateful people, furthermore, did not ignore or deny negative aspects of life. (McCullough, Emmons, and Tsang, 2002)

Feeling gratitude for opportunities, positive experiences and kindness from others allows us to savor the good times and realize that hard times are normal and usually temporary. Gratitude helps us to realize that there are valuable lessons in the mistakes we make. It teaches us that if we have everything we need, we have little to strive for or look forward to. Gratitude is humility's devoted supporter. Cicero once said that "gratitude is not only the greatest of virtues, but the parent of all others."

"Jeannie"
Jeannie Angnatuk

When eating bamboo sprouts, remember the man who planted them.

—Chinese Proverb

Jeannie was born and grew up on the land as had all of her ancestors. No one ever knew exactly when she was born, they only knew

---

The story of Jeannie Angnatuk is based on an interview with her granddaughter Annie Popert. "I am honored to have the opportunity to speak about my grandmother, the woman who has had the most influence on my life. Her Spirit is always with me. As I walk towards Elderhood I am learning to practice the values she gave me. It is important that I share with others, especially my own grandchildren, so that they too can be left with the precious things my grandmother gave me."

the season. Her nomadic people, Inuit from Labrador and Nunavik followed the caribou herds, birds, seals, whales and the seasons. In the winter she lived with her family group in igloos; in the summer they lived in tents made from skins. She learned at a young age to clean skins and make parkas and boots. She had everything the land had to offer. Life was hard at times; her father was killed by a wolf when she was young, yet Jeannie was always grateful for anything she had, for the land and for the kindness of others.

Jeannie's marriage to her first husband was an arranged one; however, he died when Jeannie was just a young woman. She remarried. One day her second husband went out in his boat. When the boat returned, Jeannie found him lying dead in it. She dearly loved her husband, and his death broke her heart.

After his death, she lived in a family group with her brothers who took care of her. She was grateful to her brothers and shared anything she had with them for the rest of her life. She always talked about how they had helped her and never let any of her grandchildren forget their kindness.

Jeannie was in her midsixties when her granddaughter, Annie, was born, and Jeannie moved off the land into a community for the first time. "I was given to her before I was a year old, and she raised me," Annie said. "Sometimes we lived with my parents, and other times we lived in a little house next to my parents and brothers and sisters. She used to tell me that I was named after her mother and how important that was to her. She loved her grandchildren and had special names for all of us.

"My grandmother called my oldest brother, Johnny, Ataataga ("my father") because he had been named after her father, who had been killed by a wolf. My brother's name was given to him in honor and gratitude. He always held a special place in my grandmother's heart. Even though the world was changing, my grandmother taught her grandchildren the importance of gratitude."

Jeannie was a small, spry woman, less than five feet tall, with her black and gray hair braided around the back of her head. Annie remembered her grandmother wearing handmade dresses made of bright-colored cloth, dark navy paisley or print material. In the winter she wore pants under her dresses and always had a scarf tied around her head. She wore aprons with pockets full of treats for the children, their misplaced toys or matches to light the stove. She was always busy skinning hides, cooking or cleaning, never sitting still. "She made wonderful banik—steamed pudding—and sometimes, as a treat, she'd make plum pudding from suet, raisins and nuts. I remember going visiting to other people's homes with my grandmother. Sometimes there would be lots of music and dancing.

"I never knew my grandmother to be unkind to anyone. She was always respectful. She treated people equally and always had a kind word for children and youth. If she had something, she shared it and was grateful to those who shared with her, always speaking of their kindness when people were around. She taught me to be grateful for everything we had and to not talk unkindly about anyone. I remember when another Inuk woman in the community, who was beginning to take on the ways of the "modern culture," made unkind remarks about our Inuit food and how strong our seal meat smelled. My grandmother didn't shame or correct her; she merely replied, "Our food is very good for us. I am so grateful we have it."

Jeannie gave what she had to those who had helped her. She shared what she had and had little understanding of those who didn't share. "When my mother was an infant, there was a famine, a scarcity of animals that happens every so often," Annie said, recounting the story she had heard many times from her grandmother. "The men had left by dog team to get food from the Hudson's Bay post. My grandmother caught a fish. She fed my mother from that one fish for many days, never eating herself. She would go rabbit hunting with another woman. One day my grandmother shot a rabbit, but the other woman said she shot it. The woman took the rabbit and shared it only with her own family, which was totally against the values our people lived by. My grandmother's heart was hurt. She told me that story many times during my young life to teach me the values of gratitude and sharing. She never spoke badly about the woman, only with sadness about what she had done."

Annie was born in a tent in a blizzard in the middle of January. Her birth was difficult, and her grandmother had always been grateful to the person who had helped with Annie's birth. "My grandmother made sure I would give my *Sanajik* ("the one who made you come into the world") the first of anything I learned to make, as well as little gifts throughout my childhood. I was told to give her something hard and something soft. The hard was a reminder that there would always be hard times, and the soft was symbolic of my love for her. Even when I was an adult, my Sanajik would do a whole ritual with me when I visited her. She would hug me and say wonderful words to me. She'd tell me I was special and that she thanked God for my birth. My grandmother would witness this ritual, always beaming with joy and gratitude.

"It wasn't until I was eleven or twelve, after our community was relocated, that alcohol came to our people and began to change our way of life," Annie said sadly, "It was the first time I remember seeing people drunk, fighting and arguing, and violence. My grandmother never drank as others did in those years, and many people sought safety at her house, including young teenagers or women who needed a safe shelter from domestic violence. She fed them and shared everything she had with them. When my grandmother died, many girls and boys were named after her because she was so loved and respected. To name a child after someone is an honor because it is hoped that the child will be like the person.

"My grandmother was proud of everything I accomplished. It was important to her that I learn English in order to survive well in a world that was changing, keep the values of our Inuit culture, be grateful for everything I was given, share what I had, and always remember and honor the kindness of others. She was a gentle and compassionate woman, the most important person in my life, and I miss her."

Consciously Learning to Be Grateful

As we express our gratitude, we must
never forget that the highest appreciation is not
to utter words but to live by them.

—John Fitzgerald Kennedy

Keep a Journal of Situations, Events and Kindnesses for Which You Are Grateful

- Every night before you go to bed, write the things you were grateful for during the day in the Gratitude section of your "Values Journal." It might be for the help of a co-worker on a difficult project, the kindness of the person in the grocery line that let you in first because you had only a few items or a neighbor who shoveled the snow from your driveway. You might list something you learned from a mistake you made, the realization of a gift you have gleaned from a painful experience, or a creative idea that came to you while driving to or from work.

Teach Gratitude to Children

- Model being grateful. Talk to your children, grandchildren, nieces or nephews about the things you are grateful for, and ask them to say what they are grateful for.
- Teach children to say "please" and "thank you" when things are given to them or done for them. It is not only good manners but also an important foundation for learning empathy for others.
- Make holidays like Thanksgiving not only occasions for pumpkin pie and turkey dinner but also times to express gratitude. Make a "Thanksgiving Tree" out of construction paper or poster board (trunk and branches). Cut lots of brightly colored leaves out of construction paper. Sometime during the day, gather everyone together to express what they have been grateful for all year.

Write each expression of gratitude on a leaf. Attach the leaves on the tree; it will be a masterpiece worthy of a Vermont autumn!

- Teach your children to be thankful for what you do rather than giving in to everything they want. When they thank you for efforts on their behalf, acknowledge their thanks with a "thank you for noticing." Help them to do their part in the family without expectation of money or gifts.
- Collect beads and help your children make gratitude bracelets, necklaces or bookmarks, adding a bead for each thing they were especially grateful for that week.

Humbly Offer Gratitude for Things Often Taken for Granted

- In our fast-moving life as we work to pay the mortgage, feed our families or accumulate the possessions we believe sustain us, we too frequently focus our attention on things we *need* or *do not have* rather than spending even a brief time every morning greeting the new day with *gratitude for what we do have.*

  Discipline yourself to get up a half hour earlier in the morning. Find a quiet place to meditate on the things you have in your life. Focus on all parts of creation, each with its own duty, which are often taken for granted: the earth that "supports our feet as we walk" and gives us sustenance; "the waters of the world that quench our thirst"; the plants that sustain us and offer us their medicine; the birds that have been given "beautiful songs to remind us to appreciate life"; the four winds that "bring the change of seasons"; the enlightened teachers who offer their gifts of knowledge and remind us how to live as people in a good way;* the laughter of children and the wisdom of elders in your life. Offer gratitude for the love that exists in the world and to those who freely offer their love and kindness to others. End this time of solitude by reading over the things you have written in your journal that you were grateful for on the previous day.

**Part of this prayer is based on the* Thanksgiving Address (Ohen:ton Karihwatehkwen) *from the native people known as the* Haudenosaunee *("Six Nations of the Iroquois Confederacy").*

Humility

It is a wholesome and necessary thing for us to turn again to the earth and in the contemplation of her beauties to know of wonder and humility.

—Rachel Carson

Humility is possibly the most misunderstood of all values. Some people believe humility to be a virtue of submission or of selling oneself short. Instead, close relatives of humility are empathy, self-esteem, integrity, compassion and courage. Humble individuals are not self-effacing, but rather think of themselves as no greater and no lesser than other human beings. They have respect for their own knowledge and capabilities and know the limits of both. Humble people value their beliefs, respect the beliefs of others, and show respect and appreciation for all life. In humility, we find the courage to offer our best to others and are willing to accept feedback and rejection without being defensive or seeking retribution. Those who exemplify humility will make the effort to listen to and respectfully accept the opinions of others while having the courage to speak their own truths and stand up for their beliefs.

Many people confuse "humility" with "shame." The difference between the two is well illustrated in a quote by Carlos Castaneda about the humility of a warrior and the shame of a beggar: "The warrior lowers his head to no one, but at the same time, he doesn't permit anyone to lower his head to him. The beggar, on the other hand, falls to his knees at the drop of a hat and scrapes the floor to anyone he deems to be higher; but at the same time, he demands that someone lower than him scrape the floor for him" (*http://en.wikiquote.org/wiki/humility*).

Humble individuals have a strong sense of self, are self-aware and able to acknowledge both their strengths and weaknesses, accept their limitations, and assume responsibility for their actions. Because of this solid and "realistic" sense of self, they are able to view others with respect and appreciate diversity, are open to new ideas, and are not defensive when confronted with feedback or opinions that are different from their own.

"Humble people," states Kenneth Hart, Ph.D., after a thorough review of research on humility, "are not at war with themselves, nor do they harbor grudges against themselves or others and have a greater level of self-acceptance of character flaws."

Without humility, it is difficult to build a compassionate world, yet perhaps more than any other value, humility is often rejected. Humility isn't a quality that comes easily to individuals or nations. We have to work hard to achieve humility. First, we must have the desire. I have been encouraged by the astounding popularity of J. K. Rowling's *Harry Potter* books, which emphasize the virtue of humility by making humility an important part of Harry's success. When Harry finds out that he is truly gifted with extraordinary talent on the Quidditch field, he neither denies nor glorifies his abilities but rather commits himself to practice harder than before.

Too many leaders and role models in our world today support the norms of "my way or the highway" and "survival of the fittest." As someone said to me when I spoke of the value of humility, "If you don't sell yourself, nobody else will. You have to look out for number one." Powerful people and nations can only win lasting respect and peace through the spirit of humility. Imposing one's own beliefs and values on another breeds violence and resistance. Everyone respectively bows to the one that bows first. Humility, rather than keeping us in chains, empowers and liberates us from false pride and arrogance. It takes security, self-esteem and courage to be humble.

"Grandma"
Mary Louise James Rapada

I long to accomplish a great and noble task,
but it is my chief duty to accomplish humble tasks
as though they were great and noble. The world is
moved along, not only by the mighty shoves of
its heroes, but also by the aggregate of the
tiny pushes of each honest worker.

—Helen Keller

Mary Louise sat at the dining room table, watching the children through the window. She loved children, and watching them play was one of her greatest joys. She had raised thirteen children of her own (seven sons and six daughters), many of her nieces and nephews, as well as countless other children in her community. Today, at the age of ninety one, she has fifty-two grandchildren and twenty-five great-grandchildren and hundreds of others that call her "Grandma."

She loved sports and rarely missed any of her grandchildren's baseball or basketball games. She'd sit in the stands and cheer them on. One game she intentionally missed was when she had a grandchild on each of the two teams playing against each other. She stayed home because she wouldn't choose which one to cheer for.

People were always coming and going in the Rapada house. Most

---

The story of Mary Louise James Rapada is based on an interview with her daughter Eleanor "Joy" Belmont. Joy states, "To us, Grandma reflects the power of the grandmother moon, the giver of life, or first teacher." Joy, too, is a wonderful reflection—a wife, mother, grandmother, great-grandmother and teacher.

of the time the house was overflowing with children. Mary never thought there were too many children. As long as she could find room, and there was always room, she would take one more. If anyone needed a place to stay, or needed care or shelter, she or he was always welcome. If people thought they were imposing, she would laugh and say, "There's always room for one more." Mary taught her children, her grandchildren and now her great-grandchildren through her example: "If you have only one piece of bread, you share it. If there are not enough beds, everybody will just have to sleep crossways. You never turn anyone away, and you always help when you are needed. Don't wait to be asked, just go."

Mary Louise had fond memories of her own childhood and of the values her large extended family taught her. She was born on March 25, 1914, on the Skway Reserve in British Columbia. She grew up on a farm and everyone fished. They had a big garden, and her mother canned all their vegetables. Her mother also taught her daughters to make cedar baskets. In May or June, the family started gathering the cedar for the baskets. They stored the cedar for a year until it aged. Each family member had a part in weaving the baskets and, when they were finished, took them into town and traded them for food, clothing and other items. They worked hard making baskets but sometimes received only a secondhand pair of shoes in exchange.

Mary married at the age of twenty-five. She was picking strawberries on Bainbridge Island in Washington State when her youngest sister's husband introduced her to a man who had come on a boat to the United States from the Philippines. She didn't like him when they first met, but she grew to love him. They were married for sixty years. She taught him how to farm. When the children were young, they worked with their parents, clearing their five-acre piece of land. Twenty-five large families lived in their community, and if someone needed a house, they would all come together to build it, followed by a big dinner and celebration. They helped each other with planting and harvesting. All the families went to the Philippine Hall on Saturday nights. They danced, talked, and celebrated a good crop, life, and the richness of family and community.

Mary always had a pot of soup on the stove and was surrounded by children. She was loving, gentle, kind and humble. She was a calm, peaceful person who never judged anyone but only quietly offered whatever she could to help. She took alcoholics into her home until they could pick themselves up again. If parents were having difficulty caring for their children, she cared for them until the parents felt able to again. She always told her grandchildren, "Don't judge others. Treat people as you would like to be treated."

In 1985, Grandma Mary was voted "Mother of the Year." As always, she was quiet, and didn't like to talk about herself. At her honoring, her children and grandchildren were there to praise her, "Our mother has spent fifty-five of her seventy years mothering, grandmothering and great-grandmothering. In one way or another, she has helped make a home for and raised every one of the seventy-three people in our immediate family. As a result, she gave up her wants and needs for her family and continues to do so."

At ninety-one, as she sits at her dining room table watching the children play, she can feel the spirit of family and community that she humbly created, living on in her children, grandchildren and great-grandchildren. In turn, her grandchildren take care of the children and elders in their communities whether or not they are related.

Today the family has once again gathered to help. One of her granddaughter Tracy's friend's father, whom Tracy called "Grandpa," has died. Tracy's husband, parents, brothers and sisters come together to make a list of what is needed and what needs to be done to support her friend's family at this time of loss. They are quietly and humbly supporting each other, the extended family, friends, and community members, just as their grandma did.

Mary Louise James Rapada bestowed upon her community and future generations a treasure chest of unspeakable wealth and priceless jewels through the time and love she gave to her family and community. "Humility is found in a vast ocean of still waters, which run very deep. At the bottom lies self-esteem. . . . One searching his or her inner world can find jewels buried in the depths. And the jewel buried deepest—which shines the brightest and gives the most light—is humility. At the darkest moments, its rays penetrate. It removes fear and insecurity and opens up the self to universal truths" (*www.livingvalues.net*).

Practicing Humility

True merit, like a river, the deeper it is,
the less noise it makes.

—Edward Frederick Halifax

Accept Yourself, Warts and All

- Give yourself the gift of allowing yourself to take an honest and courageous self-inventory. In the Humility section of your "Values Journal," list your strengths and weaknesses. After examining each strength and weakness, ask yourself if you tend to boast about your attributes and accomplishments or become defensive about your limitations and mistakes.

Search for an Honest Mirror

- Ask someone who knows you well if they would be willing to be a mirror to give you feedback regarding the way you present yourself to others and move through life. Do you show respect for the opinions and beliefs of others? Do you truly listen when another is speaking, or are you more focused on yourself in conversations and interactions? Do you show respect for the environment, or do you abuse it? Do you appreciate the differences in others, or do you present yourself and your opinions with a kind of "my way or the highway" judgment? Pay attention to how you accept the feedback from your mirror. Thank the person for his or her feedback; it is the greatest gift another can give you.

Determination

Your opponent, in the end, is never really
the player on the other side of the net, or the
swimmer in the next lane, or the team on the other
side of the field, or even the bar you must high-jump.
Your opponent is yourself, your negative
internal voices, your level of determination.

—GRACE LICHTENSTEIN

There's never been a Tour de France victory by a cancer survivor before me. That's what I'd like to be remembered for," said Lance Armstrong. He became the first cyclist to win the Tour de France seven consecutive years.

Determination is the quality of "continuing to try to do something even when it's difficult" (Longman, 2002). Throughout history, people, like the founders of Mothers Against Drunk Drivers, have been determined to stand up for others who could not speak for themselves and have turned their own personal pain into positive action. The world has also reaped the benefits of those determined people who have accomplished what they were told they couldn't, who refused to be victims and who have believed in themselves enough to achieve their dreams.

I will never forget two classmates I had early in my life. Both had been blind from birth. One spent most of her waking hours barefooted. It was as though she could see through the soles of her feet and the white cane she always carried. She could go from class to class faster than any of us, and she was an A student. Once, when walking across the campus, a well-meaning student tried to lead her. She thanked the student for her kindness and then said, laughing, "I'm blind but I'm not disabled." I asked her how she had become so incredibly independent. She replied, "My family supported me, loved me, let me make mistakes and believed I could do anything I set my mind to. Sometimes they let me fall, knowing that I would always get back up more determined than before. 'Can't' never did anything. I'm a 'can' person."

The second blind classmate was, sadly, truly "disabled" not by her lack of sight but rather by her lack of belief in herself and what she could accomplish. Her very loving and well-meaning family anxiously hovered around her, doing things for her that she was capable of doing for herself. She used her lack of sight as an excuse for poor grades, frequent temper tantrums and bullying of other students.

My grandmother and these two classmates taught me more about determination than a library full of books and reminded me of a wonderful quote by Confucius: "Our greatest glory is not in never falling but in rising every time we fall."

"Grandma Jessie"
Jessie Wartinbee

In the midst of uncertainty, keep determination in your thoughts and it will become a guiding light in front of you.

—Dadi Janki

Jessie was my grandmother . . . well, not really, but in the heart where it counts she was. All of my grandparents had died before I was born, and Jessie had been my maternal grandmother's best friend. She'd been there for my mother after her mother died, and she'd always been there for me.

Grandma Jesse was a liberated woman long before being liberated was fashionable. She outlived four husbands and her only child, was in *Who's Who of American Women* and had been crippled from polio since childhood. Jessie would have said that she was "physically challenged" not "crippled" long before the term was "politically correct." She actually asked me to help her "run away" from a nursing home (as she would always refer to the day she left) when she was eighty-five because "they" wouldn't let her eat cheese,

---

Jessie Wartinbee was my adopted grandmother. Her heart gifts were immeasurable and her determination "stands me up" and gives me courage at those times when I most need strength of mind and heart.

a primary staple of her diet for her entire life, and treated her like "an old woman." The medical staff thought that eating cheese in the ample quantities she consumed was bad for her cholesterol levels. They said she was "stubborn"; she said she was "determined."

I remember Grandma Jessie sitting on the porch in her wheelchair, tending her rose garden with the aid of her walker and making oatmeal cookies that awaited me in the red apple cookie jar on the kitchen counter. But most of all, I remember the stories she told that taught lessons I live by to this day.

One day when I was fourteen, she saw me staring at my favorite picture of her standing next to her first husband and holding her infant son in her arms. I knew the beautiful, old-fashioned long dress hid her leg braces, and I knew that her husband must have been holding her erect in the old photograph. She looked proud and happy and every bit the beautiful, fine lady she had been.

"You've never asked me about my son," Grandma Jessie said in her typical matter-of-fact way. It was true, I hadn't. I had always been curious, but I didn't want to cause her pain by bringing up bad memories. Even then, I didn't quite know how to respond to her statement.

She seemed to understand my discomfort and continued. "He died when he was three. His name was William, after his father. We called him Billy. He drowned in the pond in the backyard of our home. I had been working at my desk when I looked up from my work and glanced out the window just as he fell into the water. I thought his nanny was right there and would pull him out any second. Tragically, she had left him alone while she went into the house for a few minutes. I started screaming for her and tried to get outside in my wheelchair. By the time she got to him, it was too late. It seemed like a long time, but it was only a few minutes; that's all it took to forever change my life.

"Billy's death was the worst thing that happened to me in my life.

I didn't think I'd live through it. I blamed myself, cursed my polio and my legs that wouldn't move. I even cursed God for the first and only time in my life. I think for a while I wanted to die. I cried like I'd never stop. I couldn't work and was distant from Billy's father. I thought he blamed me, too. It's funny how our guilt plays tricks with our minds. Then one day I got up, put my feet back on the ground and started walking the road I was given. It's a good thing, too. You know what was waiting for me just around the bend?"

"What?" I was awed by her strength and determination.

"Your mother. Then around another bend, you were waiting. You've been one of the greatest blessings in my life. Sometimes life will knock you down; other times miracles lift you high. Billy's life, as short as it was, was a miracle. Most people who had polio were not blessed with a child. Then his death knocked me down. If I'd have stayed down, I truly would be crippled and would have denied myself the blessings around the bend.

"When I leave this world, I want to have no regrets. I want to know that I have walked the full length of the road I have been given, felt everything I was meant to feel, learned every lesson I could about myself and life, and fully experienced everything I have been offered. There is nothing you can't do, dear girl, nothing you can't be or get through if you set your mind to it. Remember that, and never be afraid to ask questions—that's how we learn."

Grandma Jessie walked a long road and whispered in my ear the last time I saw her, "I have no regrets." She died in her own home six months after she had turned one hundred years old. She always said she'd make it past one hundred.

Whenever one of life's challenges knocks me down, I think of Grandma Jessie standing proudly, cane in hand, and I pick myself right back up and keep going.

Strengthening Your Determination

If you think you are too small to be effective, you have never been in the dark with a mosquito.

—Unknown

Facing Challenges with Determination

- List the times in your life that you have faced challenges in the Determination section of your "Values Journal." The challenge might have been undertaking a new subject area in school, the first day on a new job, dealing with a learning disability, running a race, grieving the loss of a relationship or the death of a loved one, and so on. After each challenge, write the way you faced the challenge. Did you procrastinate, blame others, give up, grieve and move past it, hold resentments, show determination? Is there a pattern in the way you face a challenging situation? If there were times you have given up, what were the things you told yourself along the way? If you held resentments, what purpose did these resentments serve? If you accepted the challenge with determination, what were the messages you gave yourself that allowed you to succeed?

Find Role Models for Strengthening Determination

- Frequently, the way we face challenges is determined by the role models we have or have had in our lives. For instance, Grandma Jessie modeled the belief that there was little that I couldn't accomplish in my life if I was determined to meet the challenge. List in your journal those people in your life who model determination. What can each of these role models teach you about facing challenges in your life? If you cannot think of any role models, ask your friends or find role models in books or on the Internet who have faced challenges.
- If you are the role model for children—your own or others—ask yourself if you are modeling determination. How are you using words and behavior to teach them to meet challenges?

Value TEN

Self-Discipline

With self-discipline, all things are possible.
Without it, even the simplest goal can
seem like the impossible dream.

—THEODORE ROOSEVELT

"I've always wanted to be in a band," my twelve-year-old seatmate commented on our lengthy flight to Chicago. "I'd love to play the drums like some of these guys," he said, pointing to his earphones. "They're really something else." He had been thoroughly involved in his music since our flight took off, tapping the beat of each song with a pencil on the arm of his chair.

"Do you play the drums?" I asked.

"I did for a while, but couldn't get the hang of it. Now I'm trying to play the bass, but it's not working out very good either. It's really kind of boring. I think I'm going to try the guitar. I'd love to play like Hendrix. He was really something."

"How long did you play the drums?" I asked.

"About six months on and off," he said. "I really tried. My mom put out a lot of money for that set of drums."

"And the bass?" I asked

"It's been about the same," he replied sadly.

I suggested to him that he read up on Jimi Hendrix before he tackled the guitar and that he pay close attention to how long it had taken his hero to develop his talent. This young man had the dream and maybe even some musical gifts. Without self-discipline, however, he would never make his dreams a reality.

He, like many people in our culture today, wants instant success, happiness, wealth and talent. Many get angry that they aren't on top of the corporate ladder without first stepping on the bottom rung. The need for instant gratification is one of the major reasons people sometimes fail to realize their dreams. Those who are successful in art, relationships, music, running a business, farming and other ventures have one thing in common: self-discipline. They not only have the idea or the dream but also the follow-through.

How many of us have sought instant gratification at the cost of long-term success? Researcher Michael Mischel, in the well-known Sandford University Marshmallow Study, tested self-discipline and its contribution to long-term success.

Mischel gathered several four-your-olds and told them they could each have a marshmallow. He explained that if they waited to eat their marshmallows until he got back, about twenty minutes later, he would give them an additional marshmallow.

Roughly one-third ate their marshmallow as soon as Mischel left. Another third waited a short time before eating their marshmallow. The remaining third waited for Mischel's return—and received an extra marshmallow.

These children were followed through their school years and beyond. Those who sought "immediate gratification" ended up being "more troubled, stubborn and indecisive," among other negative behaviors. But those children who waited to eat their marshmallows until Mischel returned demonstrated "the habits of successful people." They were "more positive, self-motivating . . . [had] successful marriages, better health" and had "greater career satisfaction. . . ."

Self-discipline is the ability to make yourself do things you know you should do when you don't want to. It is the ability of individuals to be true to their dreams and beliefs and to give up instant pleasure and satisfaction in favor of a higher goal. Self-discipline requires patience and the willingness to make mistakes and overcome obstacles that might appear along the way to a goal. Albert Einstein once said, "I think and think for months and years. Ninety-nine times, the conclusion is false. The hundredth time, I am right." Einstein was a brilliant man who was aware that intelligence without self-discipline is only intelligence.

Because of self-discipline, an artist paints a masterpiece, an athlete wins a competition, the farmer is up before the sun rises, and ethical people hold on to their ethics and sense of self. The achievement of anything of value requires discipline. The outcome of self-discipline is self-esteem, joy, health and freedom.

"Grandma Lane"
Eva Lane

There are no shortcuts to any place worth going.

—Beverly Sills

Carrying the big pitcher of ginger water and the stack of glasses, Eva Lane stopped at the bottom of the field, not because the pitcher was heavy, although it was, but because she never tired of the sight before her. All eight of her grandchildren were in the field, the older ones helping with the haying and watching out for the younger ones, and the little ones, even little Susie still in diapers, tagging along. She couldn't think of a more beautiful sight on this sunny Vermont summer day: green fields, blue skies, the smell of freshly cut hay and those beautiful little angels. She loved every one of them. "Life is good; it is good," she thought.

She walked on and soon was surrounded by two giggling granddaughters, Tammy and Terri, still laughing at the joke their grandma had played on them the day before. She had been plucking a chicken for Sunday dinner. When she was sure that each of her grandchildren were watching, she reached in and pulled an egg out of the half-plucked chicken. Their eyes went wide with wonder; then they collapsed laughing. They loved their grandmother and the way she made even the most unpleasant job fun.

Eva Lane was born in Vermont in 1901 and, like her children and grandchildren, grew up on a farm. She married young and had eight

---

The story of Eva Lane is based on an interview with Tammy and Terri Picard. Tammy states, "Without the values of my grandmother I wouldn't be where I am today." Terri adds, "She has given her children the values she learned and she sees her children passing them on."

children, four girls and four boys, and felt pride in every one of them. When adults, all but one of her children still lived close by, and she felt blessed to see her grandchildren every day. One of her daughters had moved to New York, but came home frequently.

Her granddaughters worked with her in the garden and helped her can and make bread. Her husband, sons and grandsons hunted and trapped, so there was always plenty of moose, deer and wild turkey for her to put up for the winter. They had chickens for eggs and meat and pigs for bacon, ham and sausage. Eva worked hard from morning until night and never complained.

She loved seeing her accomplishments at the end of the day: the jars and jars of succotash, dandelion greens and vegetables from the garden sitting on the shelves of her pantry; homemade bread fresh from the oven and ready for breakfast the next morning; and always plenty of fudge, cakes and pies. She lived off the land her entire life and knew that if you were disciplined, worked hard and were good to the land, it would be good to you.

"We always loved Sunday dinners at Grandma Lane's house. There were so many people crowded in that kitchen, it was hard to move," Tammy said. "The house was always open to us and to everybody else. Nobody was ever turned away at any time, and there were always a couple extra plates set at the dinner table on Sunday for anyone in the community who might stop by. Grandma loved to cook and would share whatever she had," Terri said fondly. "She knew everybody. Besides working on the farm, she also drove the school bus when we were little. She was short, only four feet eleven, but she never let her size stop her. She just put a box there so she could work the gas and the brakes. All the kids loved her. She was one of those happy-go-lucky people and was always right there when anyone needed her."

When her grandchildren were still young, Grandma and Grandpa Lane sold the farm for pennies on the dollar to Tammy and Terri's family, and moved to a little house across the road. Still they always had Sunday dinner at Grandma Lane's house, as small as it was. "She'd have a fit if someone came over and there wasn't something homemade to eat. She was always feeding people. When she heard someone come onto the porch, she'd prepare to feed and welcome them no matter who they were or what their ages. I never heard her say that she was tired, and she never complained. Sometimes I couldn't believe all the work she could get done," Tammy said. "She'd always say it just had to be done, and she loved it. I know few people today with the kind of self-discipline she had.

"When she was in her sixties, she took on another job, cooking at a café downtown. When she came home at night, she'd always have a big bucket of compost for the pigs. We'd see her coming down the road after work, and we'd run out to meet the car, always yelling, 'Grandma Lane's here. Grandma Lane's here!' We loved her so much.

"Throughout our entire lives, I never remember being bored like kids say they are today. We'd always run around with our cousins and visit each other's houses. All of Grandma Lane's kids had big families like she did. We'd play down by the brook or pick berries, dandelions or buttercups in the summer and fall, sled in the winter, help plow in the spring, hay or help Grandma in the garden in the summer. She didn't have to ask, we just did it. We were always in the garden, in the pasture, cooling off in the brook, or running around in the barn. People were in and out of Grandma's house all day. All the adults would go to dances up at the big barn by the dam on Saturday nights. We celebrated together and worked together.

We played hard and worked hard. Grandma cared about how we were and what we were doing and tried to guide us in the right direction. Twenty-five or more of us would get together every Sunday for dinner: parents, grandparents and cousins. There was always a big roaster full of baked beans."

Eva Lane's husband went deaf in his early sixties and died at the age of seventy-one—Eva was in her late sixties when he died. In her early seventies she married a man she had met at the café. "They were always holding hands, smooching and hugging," Terri said. "We just couldn't believe it. As old as she was, she always seemed young and full of energy. She never let anything get her down.

"Grandma Lane died when she was eighty-three. We still miss her," Tammy and Terri said. "She taught us to love life, to be self-sufficient and self-disciplined, to take care of things that needed to be taken care of, and to never let anything get us down for long. She taught us by example the importance of family and community, to always be kind, and to share whatever we have with others. Her values still live on inside us today."

Developing Self-Discipline

Talent without discipline is like an octopus on roller skates.
There's plenty of movement, but you never know if
it's going to be forward, backward or sideways

—H. Jackson Brown, Jr.

Reach the Goals You Set for Yourself

- Think of a goal you want to achieve. This may be something you attempted to achieve in the past or an entirely new goal. Follow these steps in reaching your goal.
    1. Define Your Goal: Don't confuse goals with wishes. Goals are specific, not vague. Write your goal in the Self-Discipline section of your "Values Journal."
    2. Make Your Goal Realistic and Reachable: Sometimes we set goals for ourselves that are self-defeating. For example, to say you want to lose fifty pounds in two weeks is neither realistic nor reachable. It is self-defeating.
    3. Create a Meaningful Purpose: Goals that encompass an important purpose provide the motivation to work hard to accomplish the goal. For instance, I want to stop smoking because the cough I have every day is frightening, and I want to live a long life. Or I am losing friends because I haven't kept commitments; therefore, I want to start being on time when I meet my friends. Make sure the purpose is in your heart, not something you are doing based on another's opinion or to please someone else. Write your purpose under your goal in your journal and on a separate piece of paper that you carry with you.
    4. Find a quiet place, relax, close your eyes and imagine yourself having reached your goal. Imagine how you will feel. What have you gained? Is

there anything you've lost? Are you willing to let go of self-defeating behavior to reach your goal?

5. Write down a personal mantra in your journal you will use to strengthen your self-discipline in meeting this goal. For instance, "I can change anything I want to in my life. I am in control of my life. I am not going to allow outside circumstances or negative self-talk to keep me from reaching my goal. The goal belongs to me and no one else. I am in control of and responsible for my life." Read the mantra out loud when you get up in the morning and before you go to bed at night.
6. Write down ways you could possibly sabotage yourself. These may be situations or people that have kept you from reaching your goals in the past. Write solutions for each of the points you have listed.
7. Find Role Models to Help You Reach Your Goal: If your goal is to stop smoking, seek out someone you trust and respect who has stopped smoking and ask him or her to be a support to you in reaching your goal.
8. Plan the Steps You Will Take in Reaching Your Goal: If your goal is to get into better physical shape, design a reasonable exercise plan that allows you to increase exercise as you go along. Perhaps one of the steps you outline might involve a consultation with a personal trainer.
9. Be Persistent: Say to yourself, "No matter how long it takes or how hard it is, I can do it. Reaching my goal is worth it, and nothing that is really worth having comes easy."
10. Don't Get into All-or-Nothing Thinking: In other words, if you don't exercise one day, don't throw in the towel and convince yourself that you've failed. Focus on the last three days you did follow your plan, and commit yourself to following your plan tomorrow.
11. Celebrate Small Successes: Find ways to celebrate your successes along the way. Treat yourself to something small you have wanted to do or some other reward.

12. Yeah! You Did It! Know that your success came as a result of your self-discipline. You mastered your mind, emotions and body. You endured monotony, discomfort and drudgery. Celebrate the freedom that comes from self-discipline. Add your success to the Gratitude section of your journal.

Acceptance

Once you have faced the seriousness
of your loss you will be able to experience
the wonder of being alive.

—Robert Veninga

Acceptance is a major quality of resilient people. It is the ability to grieve life's tragedies or the imperfections in ourselves, acknowledge them and get on with the business of living. "God grant me the serenity to accept the things I cannot change, the courage to change the things I can, and the wisdom to know the difference" is the edict of *The Serenity Prayer* by Reinhold Niebuhr.

Acceptance is one of the hardest tasks of any recovery process: acceptance of our losses, our strengths, our behavior and the hurts we have caused others and recognition of our imperfections, the imperfections of others and of our world.

Without acceptance, we can become lifelong victims, prisoners to our imperfections. We then are bound to a painful past, repeating the behavior again and again, rather than learning from it, changing, growing and moving forward.

Sometimes we must struggle with what has been and then begin living life as it is. Those who resist change find it difficult to experience happiness. Acceptance allows us to reap the gifts during times of unfulfillment, unhappiness and profound discomfort. Sometimes the loss of a job, although painful, opens up a new career, or a painful divorce teaches us things about ourselves that make our next relationships more honest, open and meaningful.

Acceptance means more than grieving and moving beyond painful experiences. It involves recognizing that we are not perfect and learning to live with our imperfections—owning them without devaluing them. Acceptance of others and life events are largely determined by our acceptance of ourselves, our strengths and limitations. When we practice acceptance, we acknowledge that life might not always be what we want it to be; our choice is how we deal with it.

Many have diminished this important value because they have confused acceptance with submission. Far from being submissive, those who practice acceptance are compassionate and courageous. "Acceptance is complex. It is a process that may take a long time. It involves all of us, our mind, our body, our emotions, and our behavior. It is a courageous process. It is the journey of the heart" (Deegan, 1996).

"Nanny"
Katerina Cassatorie Panzica

You must shift your sail with the wind.

—Italian Proverb

"You are a no Mr. Straight, you are a Mr. Crooked," Katerina yelled in her thick Italian accent as she picked up a broom and chased the man out of her house. Her daughter had been injured in an accident at the factory, and Mr. Straight, a lawyer representing the factory, had come to Katerina's house to offer her daughter a very small compensation when the severe back injury deserved considerably more. Katerina was a warm, accepting person, yet she was definitely not submissive. She was quite capable of standing up for herself and her family. Her family had always been the center of her world.

Katerina Cassatorie Panzica was born in 1890 in Rossetano, a little town in Sicily. She was the oldest girl of seven siblings. When she was seventeen, her family arranged her marriage to a man she had only briefly encountered while walking to church with her family. Giacomo, thirteen years her senior, had seen her many times walking on the road toward the church and was smitten by this young woman. He asked her parents if he could marry her. Katerina didn't know him and didn't love him, but as was the custom in Sicily at the time, she honored her parents' wishes and

---

The story of Katerina Cassatorie Panzica is based on an interview with Georgine Dellisanti. Georgine writes: "It is clear to me, and my siblings and cousins, that my grandmother's presence, warmth, humor and well-timed words made a strong impression on all of us. The depth of the gifts she offered are more apparent to me as I age. I am fortunate to have had her in my life and pleased to have this opportunity to honor her."

married him in April 1907. Three months later, following her new husband's desires, she immigrated to the United States, leaving her family and everything she knew and held dear. She never again saw the family she loved.

When Katerina came to the United States, she knew nothing of the language or customs. They immigrated through Ellis Island and moved first to St. Louis, Missouri, to be with Giacomo's brother. A year later, they moved to New York City. Her five children were born in the city. At some point, as was true of many Italians at that time, they moved to Hillside, New Jersey, a little town outside of New York City. Giacomo was a shoemaker. They had a store, which included a shoe shop where he made and repaired shoes. Their little home in Hillside was extremely important to Katerina. By this time she could speak, read and write English, the language of her new country, and she had become a United States citizen.

Unfortunately, Giacomo was an alcoholic and the Depression was beginning to hit the United States. People were not able to pay for shoes or shoe repairs, and Giacomo, being a warm-hearted man, let them have shoes and items from the store without paying. His drinking increased, and they soon lost the house. Katerina was devastated. Yet, as with other things in her life, she grieved the loss, accepted it and prepared for yet another change.

"When my mother was thirteen," Katerina's granddaughter Georgine said, "my grandmother, mother and two older siblings went to work in a factory. My grandfather was becoming increasingly ill, so my grandmother tended to him and supported the family. She worked in the factory and took in laundry and sewing. My grandfather died five years later.

"I remember during my 'hippie' days I had long hair and patches on my clothes as was the style. My grandmother would look at me with curiosity and tell me about the days when they were poor. She told me she had taken great care to sew the necessary patches inside the garments so they wouldn't show. She was never judgmental, only curious.

"My grandmother was one of the few people in my life that I could really talk to. She thought it was wonderful that I could date young men and choose whom to marry. Although her husband was a 'good' man, she never knew if she loved him because she knew no one else. She was never bitter or negative about her life. She would always talk about things with great acceptance and quiet strength. She told us many stories about herself and her life, but there was never the slightest resentment, only teachings.

"I remember one time when my cousin was able to go to Italy and visit our relatives. She called my grandmother from her sister's house, a sister my grandmother hadn't seen since she was seventeen. I remember my grandmother saying her sister's name again and again. 'Angelina, Angelina,' she sobbed. I knew then the tremendous grief my grandmother must have gone through, leaving her family behind, yet there was never any resentment or bitterness in her. As was her way, she mourned it, accepted it and moved on. Her manner and the way she lived taught us acceptance. She never lectured, just showed us by the way she lived and met life's many challenges. The one thing she would tell us was: 'It takes courage to live a life.'"

Katerina's grandchildren remember that there was always much warmth, coziness and laughter in their "Nanny's" small apartment. She had a dog named Skippy that they played with. They remember the cookies waiting for them when they stayed with her. She patiently taught them how to make pasta from scratch and took pictures of them proudly holding up the pasta they'd made for all to see.

"Nanny was so cozy and warm," Georgine remembered fondly. "I remember sitting on her lap and leaning back into the softness of her body. I felt so warm, protected and safe. She was a big woman with long hair that she never cut. It was pulled back into a bun, very grandmotherly. She gave us something more than we got from our mothers: an incredible unconditional love, warmth and acceptance. She was the matriarch of the family, but a gentle matriarch who pulled her family around her. She was never overbearing. She would find delight in the smallest things, and we always wanted to be with her.

"On holidays the men would watch the sports games in another room, and the women would sit around this big table and laugh, talk and drink tea—three generations of us. I will always remember the warmth, laughter, and the comforting feeling of acceptance and belonging. It is deep inside my being, at the very core of my being today."

Katerina's grandchildren never heard Nanny complain. She was never negative about the circumstances of her life but instead turned them into teachings. She never questioned the events of her life or the "should haves" or "could haves." She didn't talk about God or religion, but they knew she used her rosary beads every day. "Only once did I hear her question the order of her life," Georgine said. "It was when her son, my uncle, died. She questioned why she was still alive and her son, in his fifties, had died so young. Yet as always, she grieved, accepted and moved on.

"I saw her wrestle with her own cancer for many years. Until her seventies when the cancer was diagnosed, I never saw her sick a day in her life. She died in her mid-eighties. I remember visiting her in the hospital before she died. As always, she never complained, just accepted and prepared for yet another change."

Katerina wasn't a drinker, but every Christmas she received a bottle of apricot brandy that lasted for the entire year. She gave each of her grandchildren a tiny drink and taught them how to toast each other. "I remember when she died," Georgine said, "all of us—friends and family—got together and got a bottle of apricot brandy. We toasted her and the warm and loving memories. We toasted her courage and her powerful presence in our lives. We toasted her modeling of acceptance of hard times. She taught us to value the simple things in life and the way things are, good or bad, painful or joyful. We toasted the wonderful gifts of the heart she gave us to keep inside and remember."

The Gifts of Acceptance

What the caterpillar calls the end of the world,
the Master calls the butterfly.

—Richard Bach

Lessons from Hard Times

- Think of a time in your life when you experienced difficulty, worked through the pain and were able reach acceptance and then move beyond it. In the Acceptance section of your "Values Journal," describe that time and the process of letting go. List the gifts and lessons you gained from that experience.

Difficulty with Letting Go of Pain and/or Resentments

- Now think of a difficult time in your life that you are still holding on to. What is it that makes that time difficult to accept and move forward in your life? Is holding on to the pain and/or resentment protecting you in some way? What do you need to do to reach acceptance? What might you gain if you reach acceptance and move beyond it?

Empower Yourself Through Self-Awareness and Self-Acceptance

- We empower ourselves first through self-awareness, then self-acceptance. Make a list of your strengths. If you have difficulty with this list, ask those who know you best to add strengths you may have left out. Do you have difficulty feeling pride in your strengths or accepting compliments from others? Do you deny these parts of yourself? How can you begin to acknowledge your strengths?
- Now make a list of your perceived imperfections or those parts of you or your behavior that you have had difficulty owning and accepting: a particular feature, your weight, your height, the way you laugh, your family background, something you have done to another or yourself that you have not been able to make peace with, and so on. What will you need to do to accept these attributes? For

instance, if you have difficulty accepting your culture, you might begin to read about your cultural identity and the gifts your culture has given to the world. If you have difficulty accepting your weight, decide what you want to do about it. Perhaps you could consult a physician for a healthy eating plan and exercise program. Also, if you have developed a "Barbie doll" view of beauty, check out books of art through the ages, and look at the historical view of beauty rather than the inappropriate view we seem to be inundated with today.

Courage

Courage is the price that life exacts
for granting peace. The soul that knows it not,
knows no release from little things; knows
not the livid loneliness of fear . . .

—Amelia Earhart

A boy in Boston rescued a friend who was being attacked by a dog. John Novotny, a high school student, followed his dream to be the best blind cross-country skier in the world. A seventy-year-old man risked his own life to save two women from a blazing building.

We hear of countless heroes every day who go into unknown circumstances with faith and courage. Someone who is courageous does what needs to be done even when afraid. Courage is shown when people risk their own lives to help others as was evidenced by those heroic individuals in the 9/11 tragedy, the December 2004 tsunami and the Oklahoma City bombing. We demonstrate courage by facing the truth, admitting mistakes and/or being willing to try new things.

The world is becoming a kinder and safer place in which to live because thousands of individuals have been willing to share their stories and speak the truth about intolerance, alcoholism and drug abuse, sexual abuse, community violence, and injustice even when faced with ridicule or punishment.

A young Pakistani woman, who the local press in Pakistan named Mukhtar Mai, "respected big sister," was gang-raped by four men after a village council sentenced her to this as punishment for her fourteen-year-old brother's association in public with a girl from a rival tribe. The rape of this young woman was committed as a means to punish her brother and shame the family by ensuring that Mukhtar Mai would be outcast and never marry. "Expected to kill herself, Mukhtar Mai instead fought for the rights of Muslim women. . . . A special anti-terrorism court sentenced the four accused rapists as well as two members of the panchayat court to death" (McElroy, 2005, 1–2). Mukhtar Mai was given police protection and a small compensation of a little over $8,000, which she used to open a school for the children of her village.

Courage is the act of caring for yourself or others even when it involves risk. We are not born with courage or fear. Both are brought on by our experiences over time. Fear and worry or doubt and indifference can paralyze us and cause us to go through life surviving but not living. Fear of what others might do or say can cause us to become prisoners of our thoughts. Just as horses hesitate to cross even a shallow stream because of their fear of water, many of us are paralyzed by ordinary things, while others courageously face their fears. It takes courage to care about others, to allow ourselves to be loved, to be gentle, to experience and show our feelings, to stand alone and to sometimes lean on others. It takes courage to speak the truth, stand for one's principles and fight injustice.

After World War II, two Japanese grandmothers set up a camp at the foot of Fuji, a sacred mountain of their people occupied by the United States military. They stood in front of guns during military exercises and shouted to the soldiers, "'Shame on you. You should go home to your mothers.' This so unnerved the young men that they could not fight. The police finally came, twelve men with shields and battle armor, to arrest the two old women. Even after the women left, the troops were spooked and could no longer desecrate the mountain with their war games. Life is stronger than death" (Bertell).

History has shown incident after incident where grandmothers were willing to stand in front of guns to protect their grandchildren, burial grounds, and sacred areas of their culture and people. For most of us, our daily acts of courage are perhaps less magnanimous but by no means trivial. Many people stand up for their beliefs, make changes in their small part of the world, have the courage to speak truth when it is more popular to keep silent, or stand up for their principles or the health and well-being of children and grandchildren without ever receiving the praise or recognition for their courage.

"Ma Linny"
Lillian Johnson

To reach for another is to risk involvement.
To expose your feelings is to risk exposing
your true self. To place your ideas, your dreams,
before a crowd, is to risk their loss. To love is to risk
not being loved in return. To live is to risk dying.
To hope is to risk despair. To try is to risk failure.
But risks must be taken, because the greatest hazard in
life is to risk nothing. . . . They may avoid suffering
and sorrow, but they cannot learn, feel, change, grow,
love, live. Chained by their attitudes, they are
a slave, they have forfeited their freedom.
Only a person who risks is free.

—Anonymous Chicago Teacher

Lillian Johnson stepped out of her house on the way to the grocery store. She was five feet one, in her late sixties and had hair the texture of dandelion fluff. This morning, however, instead of her hair being its normal bright white, it was metallic purple. Something had gone terribly wrong with the blue rinse she used to brighten her normally white hair. Shoulders back, head high, she strode along the street, seemingly oblivious to the stares that came

---

The story of Lillian Johnson is based on an interview with her grandson, Jeff Lindholm. Jeff is a book copyeditor and freelance writer living in Vermont. "I have also sung in a punk rock band, led troubled youth on wilderness trips, worked in a record store and poured concrete for sidewalks. I get my work ethic and my sense of humor from my grandmother."

her way. She just nodded, smiled and walked on. She wasn't unaware of the looks from passersby, but rather had learned a long time ago to make the best of situations beyond her control, and right now her purple hair was beyond her control. The beautician she consulted said that she could set it right in a couple of weeks, so she would just go about her business until then. Her grandson, Jeff, had said that her purple hair had caused him to lose his appetite at dinner the night before. She laughed, getting a kick out of her grandson's dry humor. Jeff was learning from his grandmother to accept what he couldn't change and not to give so much power to what other people thought. Mistakes happen, and you just have to learn from them and make the best of it.

Lillian Johnson's parents came from Sweden in the 1880s. She was born in the United States in 1893. Their name was originally Funke but, like many family names, was changed in Ellis Island. She grew up in Mt. Jewett, Pennsylvania. Lillian became pregnant while still in high school and was married to the father of her child for only six months when both came to the conclusion that the marriage was not going to work. They decided that continuing the marriage would only cause emotional pain for their unborn child. It was a courageous act for a woman in that time to divorce and have a child on her own. Her son, who was born shortly following the divorce, was the only child Lillian would ever have. She did anything and everything to support her child, including cleaning homes, taking in ironing and doing odd jobs.

Lillian eventually moved in with her parents and helped support them as well. Her mother ran a boarding house and took in Swedish immigrants who worked in the "cut sole" factory in the small town. "Sometimes these guys would get drunk and rowdy, and my great-grandmother would throw pepper on the potbellied stove to drive them out of the house. She was also a woman of courage," Jeff said proudly.

Lillian and her parents had a hard time surviving during the Depression. "My dad was in high school during the Depression. I always respected and admired my grandmother for her courage and hard work," Jeff said. "She cleaned houses until she was in her seventies and never complained. She went with a man for years but never married him because he was taking care of his mother, and she was taking care of hers. My great-grandmother had left the house to Ma Linny when she died. She wanted to acknowledge her kindness for taking care of her throughout her life."

Unfortunately, Ma Linny's mother had not made a will, and Lillian's sisters wanted her to sell the house and divide the money between them. Rather than create difficulties, she did as her sisters wished. She came to live with Jeff's family when he was an adolescent. Much later, her friends introduced her to a man she eventually fell in love with. She married Ed and moved out of the family's house.

Ma Linny took care of people most of her life: her son, her parents, Ed's parents and finally Ed, who had developed a lung condition from breathing the chemical fumes in the factory where he worked.

Ma Linny taught her grandson to take care of himself and the people he loved. She also encouraged him to be his own person and to have the courage of his convictions. "My parents often cared too much about 'What people would say?' but Ma Linny taught me to think things through carefully, then go for it. When I was a grown man and working in a school for delinquent youth, I started a rock band with some friends, and we played music around town. My parents were desperately afraid that the school principal would find out, and I would get fired. But the principal and all the teachers in the school knew what I was doing and thought it was cool. My parents were afraid that I'd set myself on fire. I think that came from watching a famous rock band set fire to things on TV. When the band played over the college radio station, my mother called me saying, 'Your dad's so upset!' and then my dad phoned, 'Your mom's so upset!' Ma Linny came to hear me play and commented later to my parents, 'He's having fun playing music. It's art; it's a good thing.' At one point my parents criticized me because I let my hair grow below my ears. Ma Linny said, 'For heaven's sake, what will it hurt if Jeff grows his hair below his ears?' "

Ma Linny taught Jeff to work things through, make mistakes and learn from them. "I remember once when I was a little kid, I was arguing with her about something. I told her, 'I don't like you, and I'm going to run away from home.' Instead of punishing me, she said, 'Okay, see you.' I packed a box with my GI Joes, toys, books and other things and started off into the woods. I completely forgot to bring food. I walked out into the woods where my tree house was. I stayed there for a couple of hours and started to get cold and hungry. By then it was almost dusk. I got my box and dragged it back home. I came in and apologized. She said that was good. She didn't get flustered or anything. She just let me work it through. That was it. She knew me and what I was capable of and trusted what I would do. I learned from her to trust myself and my own decisions."

When Jeff had been in college for a couple of years, he wanted to take a year off to figure out what he really wanted to do. That made sense to Ma Linny. His parents, however, were afraid that if he stopped he would never go back. To please his parents, he continued his schooling and eventually earned a degree in English. He began teaching school. Years later he went back to college for a degree in journalism, which is what he realized his passion was. Ma Linny backed him, trusted him and understood him more than his parents did. She knew that if he had taken a break from school, he would have gone back once he decided the path he wanted to take. She wanted Jeff to blossom, grow, trust himself, try things and have the courage to follow his own path. She listened to his plan and tried to convince his parents. "He does have a plan. He's making sense. He has thought things through, and you should listen to him."

"Today my willingness to jump into the deep end comes from Ma Linny. She taught me to take chances when it was important, to follow my convictions and to never live my life in worry and fear. I learned from her to make decisions wisely, then go for it. Those times when I need to stand up for myself and my beliefs or to take a risk, I feel that part of her in me, and I don't let myself be held back by fear. She always said, 'If you're afraid of doing something because you might make a mistake or displease others, think about it long and hard. If it's important, have the courage to do it. If it doesn't work out, learn from it and move on. It takes courage to live life well and to risk making mistakes. Take a chance, and go for it!' "

Facing Our Fears and Developing Courage in Our Lives

You gain strength, courage and confidence by every experience in which you really stop to look fear in the face. . . . You must do the thing you think you cannot do.

—Eleanor Roosevelt

Realistically Examine Your Fears

- In the Courage section of your "Values Journal," list the times when you let fear prevent you from doing something or you let it dictate your decisions. Examples might be that you did not stand up for a co-worker who was being bullied because you were afraid of losing your job, or you didn't try something new because you were afraid of making a mistake. Now, examine your decision from a distance. What was the worst thing that could have happened? Were your fears "realistic"? Sometimes fear is our friend and prevents us from injury. Other times it paralyzes us and stops us from living.

Change the "What If?" into "So What?"

- Worry can also be your friend. It can help you to rescue yourself or someone else who really could be in trouble. But you can't let worry run loose like a mad dog and allow it to drive you into a corner. Make a list of all of the things you worry about during the next week. Is worry keeping you safe or driving you into a corner and stopping you from becoming the courageous person you were meant to be? Try changing the "what if?" to "so what?"
- Review your list often. Refine it and applaud your courage and conviction when you have conquered your fears.

Cooperation

Snowflakes are fragile things individually,
but look what they can do when
they stick together.

—Fernando Bonaventura

Cooperation is the ability to join with others for the common good or in order to accomplish a common task. The task may be as simple as cooking a meal or as complex as challenging injustice in the world.

Over time we have developed a strong belief in individualism. When we become focused on individual efforts and concerns, we sometimes sacrifice cooperative efforts in family and community. The benefits of working together are obvious: we can accomplish much more together than alone. For instance, when carrying a big load, it helps to have someone share the burden; when attempting to reel in a huge fish, we need the help of our fellow fishermen; if we want to eat healthy food and cannot afford the steep cost of organic vegetables, we can join with our neighbors in starting a community garden. When cooperating with others, we not only accomplish more but usually feel happier, more content and secure.

The shift of focus from "we" to "me" can lead to a growing sense of isolation and a breakdown in our awareness of others. This lack of connectedness with others can diminish our sense of well-being and can put our safety and security at risk. Many violent incidents in our schools have been aborted when community members shared information and joined together to prevent situations from escalating into devastating acts of violence.

In the fifties and earlier, families often sat on the front stoops or porches during all hours of the day or night. Here they socialized, swapped stories, planned community gardens, made plans to help each other put up food for the winter or help a neighbor build a barn. People shared information about their families and kept an eye on the children. Many older adults have told me that they felt secure as children because many eyes were watching them. Children learned to be more responsible because if they did anything wrong in another part of the neighborhood, their parents would know of it before they returned home. People were acutely aware of the comings and goings of others on their block or in their communities. Sociologists actually had a name for this historical aspect of community life: Front Stoop Neighborhood Control. Cooperation allowed families to feel supported and secure. When community members look out for one another, children and families are safer.

When we cooperate with one another, individual contributions and rights are respected. Each person does his or her best and encourages others to do the same. Rather than competing or making comparisons, we appreciate the contributions of others and view mistakes as opportunities to learn. When we cooperate with one another, we are aware that we can accomplish far more together than we can alone.

"Grandma" Ida Goodleaf (Kawennotie, "Floating Words")

Now join your hands, and with
your hands your hearts.

—William Shakespeare

Six-year-old Suzy loved apples and proudly told anyone who would listen that the cold, crisp apples from her grandma's root cellar were the "best in the whole wide world." Her grandma would sit in a chair, surrounded by her grandchildren, peeling a prize apple; then she'd slice it up and share it. If all of her grandchildren were at her house, she might even bring up two apples to share. As she peeled, she captivated the eager listeners with the tale of the

The story of Ida Goodleaf is based on an interview with her granddaughter Suzy Goodleaf. Suzy is the second oldest of Ida's fifteen grandchildren. She and her partner have contributed two children to Ida's great-grandchildren. "In my work as a psychologist, I strive to follow the values instilled by my grandmother. I work for First Nations communities to help my people realize who they are, where they come from, and appreciate the history of their ancestors."

cherished apple she would find in her stocking on Christmas mornings during the long Depression. She was a wonderful storyteller, and Suzy always felt as though she were eating a slice of the very apple that had been in her grandma's stocking so long ago.

Ida Goodleaf (Kawennotie) was born in 1921, the fourth of six children in Kanewake, Quebec, a Mohawk reserve on the outskirts of Montreal. Her father was a steel worker and traveled the long distance to New York City every Sunday afternoon and would not come home until Friday night. Her family had a farm with pigs, cows, horses and a huge garden. The only part of the yard that was not covered with garden was the path where people walked. Ida's maternal uncle had a farm down the way, and the family would help weed the crops in return for planting a portion of his land. They stored the vegetables in the root cellar for the long winter.

When Ida was a year old, she contracted polio and was paralyzed. She was hospitalized for almost a year. After regaining her physical abilities, she was not allowed to play outside with the other children. Her parents had to limit her activity for many years and make certain that she got plenty of rest in order to avoid further health complications.

When Ida was ten, her father died in an accident on the job, and her mother had to support the family. She received a small insurance benefit from the accident and bought a little store on the reserve where she sold flour and basic household needs to the community. Ida and her brother and sisters pitched in and helped their mother with the store. Because she still had to limit her activity, Ida was usually the cashier. She loved listening to the stories told by community members, and in the early evenings when she was supposed to be in her bed asleep, she'd sneak into the store and hide under the counter to listen to the stories the old men told when they came in. Later, her grandchildren realized that this was where their grandmother developed her interest in the history of the people in her community and learned to be a captivating storyteller.

Suzy and her cousins and their friends loved to listen to her grandmother's stories of community life in the 1920s. She told them of the corn husk bees and the community dances that followed the the bees. She also told about the fun that families would have in the winter, sliding day and night down the hill that had been carefully tended by a neighbor. Ida made many of the beautiful dresses worn by family and community members for the "sociables" on the reserve.

Her skill as a seamstress was well-known, and she had once been asked to make outfits to be used in a movie. She had been honored and was very careful to buy beautiful leather that was very clean. She had spent hours laying out the leather to make certain there were no holes in the garments and was shocked when the crew threw her meticulously sewn creations into the dirt and stomped on them in order to make them look old and worn.

Suzy loved to go to her grandmother's house. "The house would always have wonderful, warm smells of leather. She would be at her sewing machine working the leather or doing beadwork, or she'd have a huge quilt laid out that nearly filled her entire dining and living room area. There would be lots of people sitting around a big table working on the quilt. The person having the quilt made would embroider on fabric squares. Then Ida would sew the squares together to make the top. She set a two-by-four at each end of the table and tightly wound up one side of the quilt, filler and backing over one board and clamp it to the other to stretch the quilt. Then she would lightly sketch an intricate pattern on the quilt with a pencil. Anyone who stopped by would pick up a needle and thread and stitch, following the pattern line, while they drank tea and visited. She would go around checking to make certain that there weren't any mistakes in the stitching," Suzy said. "If a mistake had been made, she'd carefully remove the stitches and we'd have to do it all over again. The expectation was that everyone would do their best all the time because the quilt was special to the person for whom it was being made. Usually, as we worked, we'd be thinking about that person or talking, joking or telling stories about her while we sewed so that thoughts of her were in every stitch. When the quilting was finished, my grandmother would bind the quilt. And then the next quilt to be made would be started by another woman in the community."

When anyone came to Ida's house, she always fed them. Whenever anyone came in, she automatically started cooking. "She'd never say anything," Suzy laughed. "She'd just start cooking. This was the signal that you were going to stay for breakfast, lunch or supper. Originally, there might have been four of us visiting, so she'd make enough for my grandpa, her and the four additional people. Then others would drop by with their families, and there was suddenly enough food for ten. I used to think it was magical that the food just seemed to multiply since there was always enough. Now I know that she would go to the fridge and get something to add to what she was making or she'd start another dish. There was also an unspoken rule that we learned very young at my grandmother's house: look around to see how many people are around the table and never take more than your share to ensure that everyone gets fed. No matter how much we ate, it was always enough. People ate with respect. She taught us to feed people and take care of them when they came to our homes no matter what time of the day or night. If there is only one cake, cut the pieces smaller, but always share."

Ida also became the "Keeper of the Books" in her community. She created a book with everyone's family tree. She carefully researched the history of everyone on the reserve. People came to her to find out who their ancient ancestors were. Community members would ask her who their great-great-great-uncle was, and she could tell them. It was important to her that people knew who their families were. Her research went back to the time when people in her community had only Indian names, long before anyone had English or family names.

She was also a chief in her community for many years. There were three women on the council with her, and they fought to make needed changes for the rights of women in their community. They fought to make changes to the Indian Act where the laws were unfair to women. For instance, in the law a Mohawk woman would lose her status if she married a nonnative and would be forced to leave the community. Mohawk men, on the other hand, could marry a nonnative and keep their status. "We are a matriarchal, not patriarchal, people," Suzy said. "It was like women were second-class citizens according to the Indian Act. My grandmother fought in Ottawa for equality for women. She could move people to cooperate in order to make change. She appealed to the integrity of others to help, and they did.

"I remember my grandmother's house as a gathering place," Suzy said. "People would always be sitting on rocking chairs on her porch, or sitting on the wide porch rail, talking and asking others to join them when they walked by: children, teenagers, adults and elders. She would always bring people together to do things and make sure that others in the community were all right. Even today many people gather at her house, talking, working on quilts, playing games—and the children are always included.

"My grandmother taught me through modeling that, as a Mohawk woman, I was to be strong, cooperate with others, share whatever I have, think before I speak, honor the elders and the children, and always be kind to people. Today I live the values my grandmother taught me and model them for my children."

Fostering Cooperation in Your Family and Community

Power can be seen as power with rather than power over, and it can be used for competence and cooperation, rather than dominance and control.

—Anne L. Barstow

Together Everyone Achieves More

- Set aside an evening for a dinner and discussion with friends and family. Ask everyone to make or bring a dish to contribute to the dinner. Children can contribute a dish, too. After dinner, gather ideas for a project that you could do together: a garage sale, a community garden, monthy progressive dinners, canning vegetables or fruits to share with each other and/or community members, making candles for holiday gifts, making quilts as Ida did with her family and community, and so on. Ask for volunteers for each task that needs to be accomplished, and set time aside for your project. Plan a celebration when each task is completed.

Learn to Ask for Help

- Many of us feel overwhelmed at times with things that need to be accomplished. Sometimes family, friends or community members would be more than willing to help, yet we don't ask, telling ourselves that we "should" be able to do it alone. Think of the times you have needed assistance and haven't asked for help. List the reasons in the Cooperation section of your "Values Journal" that prevented you from stating your needs. Reread Ida's story, paying close attention to the value of cooperation. Change the messages you give yourself. The next time you need help, ask.

Contribute Talent, Energy and Time to a Community Project

- Read the local paper for several weeks and circle community activities you feel are important: feeding the homeless at a local shelter, helping with a fund-raiser, joining a task force, supporting a candidate for office, to name a few. Set aside time to volunteer for the project you have selected, and ask family members and/or friends to join you. If you have a particular interest that is not being addressed, advertise for volunteers and start your own project.

Value FOURTEEN

Truth

We can easily forgive a child who is afraid of the dark; the real tragedy of life is when men are afraid of the light.

—Plato

Breakfast cereals promise more energy, a favorite soft drink promises freedom, and a credit card company says we'll have a 4.5 percent interest rate for the life of the loan—oops, forgot to read the really small print that says the company can change the rate at any time.

Being truthful is saying what is so, even when it is easier not to. It is saying what is true: stating the facts about something, one's true opinion; or admitting when a mistake is made and accepting responsibility for the fallout. Being truthful is often choosing a more difficult course of action. An honest person not only speaks the truth but also lives life in a genuine and authentic way. When one lives a truthful life, there are no gaps in how he acts, how he feels and what he says.

When writing about this value, I talked to many people about truth and received three general responses: (1) there is no such thing as honesty and truth anymore, (2) today everyone is out for "number one," and deception is the name of the game, and (3) I can't be responsible for the honesty of others, only my own truthfulness to myself and others. When we have lost truth, we have lost everything.

Although most people agree that truth is still an important value, there seems to be growing evidence that truth matters less today than financial success, influence and power. Many people in public office are caught in lies and accused of serving their interests rather than the interests of the people they represent. We read almost daily of the dishonest conduct and lack of integrity of CEOs and we are losing respect for religious institutions because of appalling abuse cases and misuses of power. Yet, in balance, hundreds of courageous, honest individuals with great integrity are responsible for bringing these long buried, once silent truths into the light.

"Institutions do not lie. Churches do not lie. Even governments do not lie. People do. Organizations act honestly or otherwise only because the people within them act that way. It is vitally important that we each accept a personal responsibility to an ethical way of life. . . . There needs to be a cultural awakening within institutions whether they be public, private or religious that rewards honesty not simply penalizes dishonesty" (Fitzgerald, 2004).

Many people tell me it is more difficult to practice honesty today because they are constantly being deceived. Inner peace and truth do not depend on the events taking place outside of us, nor can they be taken away because of the dishonesty around us. Blame is useless and only paralyzes us with inaction, whereas truth to oneself and others moves us forward.

Honesty is present when we care about ourselves and others. True caring involves seeing others as they are, not how we would like them to be, and disciplining ourselves to be self-aware. Honesty's closest friend is courage. When we're honest, we do not stoop to half-truths to mislead or deceive, nor do we remain silent about important issues when it is more convenient to keep our thoughts buried. It is vitally important that each person accepts the responsibility to live a life based on honesty of word and action in order to prevent greed and the pursuit of power and influence from replacing the values of truth and courage. Without a commitment to truth, it is impossible to restore trust. "To deal honestly when you were deceived, to have empathy when you were often hurt, to speak straight when you heard mostly double talk . . . requires great imagination and strength" (Wolin and Wolin, 163).

"Nana"
Eileen Moyes

Honesty consists of the unwillingness to lie to others; maturity, which is equally hard to attain, consists of the unwillingness to lie to oneself.

—Sydney J. Harris

"I'm going to make sure you lose your job for this!" the woman yelled at Doug, who had just refused to serve her a drink at the Dog and Fox, a pub outside of London. He could barely hear himself think; people laughing, dogs barking and now this customer screaming. Well, he definitely didn't want to lose his job. He pictured Nana waiting up for him when he came back to her house after work. She didn't need to remind him to be true to himself; she and the son she raised had taught him that all his life. Being true to himself tonight meant not serving a pregnant woman alcohol, whether or not he would lose his job.

Later, sitting at the old scarred kitchen table in Nana's cozy kitchen, he told her about his night. He finished the story with, "Well, I didn't lose my job. I think my boss respected me for standing up for what I believed, but he served the woman alcohol anyway. I thought maybe he would; I just couldn't do it."

"I'm proud of you," she said. "The shepherd's not the only one in the field. If you can't sleep at night, the only one you're hurting is yourself."

The story of Eileen Moyes is based on an interview with her grandson Doug Moyes. Doug would like to honor his grandmother with one of her favorite Old English proverbs: "We never know the worth of water 'til the well runs dry."

Like so many of Nana's sayings over the years, it had taken Doug a long time and a lot of thought to understand that the "other" in the field was the shepherd's conscience. Nana's lessons usually required serious thought. She never spoon-fed him values, never lectured; she modeled them and made him think. When the lessons got through, they were with him for life.

Now sitting at his own kitchen table, Doug thought of that night and so many of Nana's teachings. He laughed. He was remembering the tomatoes, another hard-won lesson. He would never forget the boiled tomatoes that Nana had served him breakfast, lunch and dinner for four days when he was staying with her as a young man of twenty. He kept leaving them on his plate but wouldn't tell her that he didn't like them because he didn't want to hurt her feelings. Then one meal the tomatoes didn't show up. "Where are the tomatoes?" he had asked. "Well," she replied, "I thought you would finally let me know that you didn't like them or you would eat them. I guess I'm giving you a chance to tell me that you don't like boiled tomatoes. It's good to be honest about what you like or don't like. Honesty is important, and everyone has likes and dislikes. It is not good to waste. If you mind the pence, the pounds will come."

Nana, Eileen Moyes, lived in the same house for over sixty years. Doug remembered her white hair and proper dress. She always wore a dress or a blouse and skirt, even when she was gardening. "Nana always looked nice. My Grandfather Fred's son married a seamstress who used to make my grandmother's clothes. She was also the seamstress for the Prime Minister's wife, Camilla Parker Bowles and Mick Jaeger's wife. Nana was proud to wear her stunning creations."

Eileen had raised her only son, Doug's father, in England during World War II. She remembered the constant air raids in Wimbledon, the village she lived in outside of London. She would grab the baby and run to the church basement down the road. Her husband was the publisher of a newspaper and traveled throughout Europe. She had been left alone much of the time and raised her son by herself. She didn't speak much of those difficult times during World War II, but Doug remembered once when visiting her that they had gone to a friend's house for dinner. He had been in the Royal Navy and spoke that night about the trauma he had gone through in the war. He and Nana cried.

Eileen's husband died when Doug's father was an adolescent. He left her a good pension, which allowed her to live in comfort for the rest of her life in the small cottage they had shared during their marriage. Eventually, she began a relationship with Fred. Although she never married him, he was the only grandfather Doug had known. By the time Fred and Eileen were together, Doug's father and mother had married and moved to the United States. His mother was Jewish and his father was Protestant. Nana had given her blessing to the union, but his mother's family didn't approve of the marriage. Nana realized that the marriage had been born out of true feelings and a great deal of thought. When he moved to the States to find peace from the pressure of his in-laws, Doug's father missed his mother terribly. She came to visit for two weeks every year, and they frequently visited her in her little house in Wimbledon.

Doug cherished the visits with Nana. "Her house was small. Everything was on a small scale. But you wouldn't believe the food that came out of that little kitchen: wonderful custards, truffles, shepherd's pie, bubble and squeak (sausages and cabbage) and, of course, boiled tomatoes," Doug laughed.

"Things were very different in England," he said. "Everything was delivered to your door: eggs, milk, fish, meat, cheese, even liquor." Then he laughed again as he remembered another of his grandmother's teachings. "Nana always ordered a bottle of gin once a week. This one delivery man tried to get something by her. He began delivering two bottles of gin a week, which Nana knew was no mistake. So she conscientiously left the money for his bill every week and saved the extra bottles that she had not ordered until she had saved twenty-three of them. Because the man delivered the liquor on his bicycle, she wanted to save enough for him to have to make several trips to take the bottles back. He never brought more than one again.

"My father, having been schooled in the consequences of dishonesty by Nana, always raised us to be honest as well. I remember once when I was about five, and my brother was three or four, my parents went out for dinner, leaving us with the babysitter who babysat most of the kids in the neighborhood. They thought they could trust her. She was drawing a bath for my brother and me when the phone rang. She had just turned on the hot water. She had been expecting a call from her boyfriend and talked with him for a few minutes, then remembered she'd left the bathwater running. She also had forgotten that she had turned on only the hot water. She undressed my brother first and then began to sit him into the water. When his little feet and bottom hit the water, he let out a scream I will never forget. He got second-degree burns on his feet and bottom as a result. He still has the scars today. When the doctor at the hospital began to treat the blisters, he told my brother that it wasn't going to hurt. My father took my brother's little hands in his, looked at him with tear-stained eyes and said, 'It is going to hurt, son, but we have to treat the burns so the pain will stop, and you can get well.' He never lied to us, just as his mother had never lied to him."

Doug's father also taught his children honesty in the same way his mother had taught him. When they didn't tell the truth, they would have to do chores to make up for the hurt they had caused by lying. They would have to weed the garden, chop wood and carry rocks. Once when Doug and his brother had accidentally broken a window while having a stone fight, they thought that their father wouldn't notice and hid the accident from him. He, of course, noticed right away, and they had to carry stones in the wheelbarrow from the back of the house to the front all day. "He made the path really long, too," Doug laughed. "We never tried to keep something from him again. We learned to be honest and take responsibility for what we did.

"Nana taught my father well, and both of them taught us. She was always direct, always got her point across and always had a teaching. She was kind, never harsh. She died at eighty-eight years of age. I miss her so much, especially at times like this when I am having a conversation about her with someone. Time just seems to fly. She was loving and kind, honest and truthful and expected me to be. Because of her teachings, I am."

Cherishing Truth in Our Lives

Honesty has a beautiful and refreshing simplicity about it. No ulterior motives. No hidden meanings. An absence of hypocrisy, duplicity, political games, and verbal superficiality. As honesty and real integrity characterize our lives, there will be no need to manipulate others.

—Chuck Swindoll

Honor Your Truth

- Think of times when you were truthful with yourself and others, even when it was difficult. Make a list of those times in the Honesty section of your "Values Journal." Find a way to honor yourself for your truthfulness. Sometimes your compassionate honesty may not be fully appreciated by another, yet it is one of the greatest gifts you can offer a friend.

Honor the Truth of Others

- Thank someone in your family and/or a friend for times when they were truthful with you about something important. Often we become defensive when others have the courage to be honest with us, and we forget to thank them for their gift when we have had time to appreciate it.

Honor Truth in Your Community

- Sit down with family and/or friends and think of community leaders or neighbors who have taken a stand and shown leadership on a controversial issue. Write a letter to them thanking them for their courage in speaking the truth. Think of making it a habit to thank people in your workplace or community for their honesty. We often punish dishonesty but seldom praise those who are truthful.

Patience

Patience is the companion of wisdom.

—Saint Augustine

Drivers honking at other drivers on the highway; caregivers yelling at children to hurry up; retirees on vacation, tapping their feet or making rude comments about the service while waiting in line at the airport. Many times I am in a rush to get somewhere, impatient with people moving "too slowly" ahead of me. I have to make myself stop and think, "What's the rush? You have plenty of time. Why are you being so impatient?"

Frequently, patience is hard work. Having patience is the ability to live fully in the present and recognize the things in life that are within our control and those that are beyond our control: what is actually within our power to change in a good way and what is not. Having patience is actively and realistically adjusting our expectations of ourselves, others and life itself. When we find ourselves being impatient, it is important to imagine a more patient, calm and serene version of ourselves and do what we must to become that person at that moment.

Impatience rarely makes things happen faster or better. The only thing our lack of patience accomplishes is to put more stress on our bodies, and pressure in our lives, cause hurt for our loved ones or create more frustration for the guy in front of us. Will it really matter if we get home five minutes later or if our child takes four minutes instead of one to tie his shoes? Hey, forget the ties, maybe we should get shoes with Velcro straps, so we don't have to wait at all. Where are we going, and what's the hurry?

Impatience adds difficulty to a situation that was not, in all likelihood, that difficult to begin with. Sir Winston Churchill once said, "When I look back on all these worries, I remember the story of the old man who said on his deathbed that he had had a lot of trouble in his life, most of which never happened."

READER/CUSTOMER CARE SURVEY

HEFG

We care about your opinions! Please take a moment to fill out our online Reader Survey at **http://survey.hcibooks.com**. As a **"THANK YOU"** you will receive a **VALUABLE INSTANT COUPON** towards future book purchases as well as a **SPECIAL GIFT** available only online! Or, you may mail this card back to us and we will send you a copy of our exciting catalog with your valuable coupon inside.

(PLEASE PRINT IN ALL CAPS)

First Name ______ MI. ______ Last Name ______

Address ______ City ______

State ______ Zip ______ Email ______

1. Gender
❒ Female ❒ Male

2. Age
❒ 8 or younger
❒ 9-12 ❒ 13-16
❒ 17-20 ❒ 21-30
❒ 31+

3. Did you receive this book as a gift?
❒ Yes ❒ No

4. Annual Household Income
❒ under $25,000
❒ $25,000 - $34,999
❒ $35,000 - $49,999
❒ $50,000 - $74,999
❒ over $75,000

5. What are the ages of the children living in your house?
❒ 0 - 14 ❒ 15+

6. Marital Status
❒ Single
❒ Married
❒ Divorced
❒ Widowed

7. How did you find out about the book?
(please choose one)
❒ Recommendation
❒ Store Display
❒ Online
❒ Catalog/Mailing
❒ Interview/Review

8. Where do you usually buy books?
(please choose one)
❒ Bookstore
❒ Online
❒ Book Club/Mail Order
❒ Price Club (Sam's Club, Costco's, etc.)
❒ Retail Store (Target, Wal-Mart, etc.)

9. What subject do you enjoy reading about the most?
(please choose one)
❒ Parenting/Family
❒ Relationships
❒ Recovery/Addictions
❒ Health/Nutrition
❒ Christianity
❒ Spirituality/Inspiration
❒ Business Self-help
❒ Women's Issues
❒ Sports

10. What attracts you most to a book?
(please choose one)
❒ Title
❒ Cover Design
❒ Author
❒ Content

TAPE IN MIDDLE; DO NOT STAPLE

NO POSTAGE
NECESSARY
IF MAILED
IN THE
UNITED STATES

BUSINESS REPLY MAIL

FIRST-CLASS MAIL PERMIT NO 45 DEERFIELD BEACH, FL

POSTAGE WILL BE PAID BY ADDRESSEE

Health Communications, Inc.
3201 SW 15th Street
Deerfield Beach FL 33442-9875

FOLD HERE

Comments

"Nana"
Corinne Chapin Titus

Patience and perseverance have a magical effect before which difficulties disappear and obstacles vanish.

—John Quincy Adams

Sue met me at the door, a toddler on her hip and two others holding on to each leg. Barking dogs and chirping birds created a homey backdrop to the evidence of children's creative play throughout the house. I knew that Sue had run a day care for twenty-seven years, much of the time while raising her own four children. Her husband had been a farmer for most of their married life and spent long hours working the land. Recently, one of her sons in the Vermont National Guard was sent to Iraq, and in addition to running her day care and pet care business, Sue was helping her daughter-in-law with her grandchildren. "Where do you get all your patience?" I asked, amazed at her calm presence.

"From my Nana," she replied smiling. "She was the most patient woman on the face of the Earth, which is unbelievable because she spent so much of her adult life as 'a lady of leisure' in New York society. She certainly wasn't that 'lady of leisure' when she was raising my brother and me. It's hard to believe that she was in her late

---

The story of Corinne Chapin Titus is based on an interview with her granddaughter Sue Hawkins. Sue writes: "As a child I did not know that my Nana would be such a big influence in my life. As an adult I know that Nana gave my brother and me a great deal: her love, her time and the expectation that we would have the strong values that she modeled when we were adults."

sixties and early seventies while raising her grandchildren. My parents were divorced. I rarely saw my father, and it seemed like my mother was never there. It was always Nana whom I could rely on. She was always a loving, patient presence."

Corinne Chapin Titus was one of the Mayflower Daughters. Her family's history traces back to the first Europeans in America. She was born in Ohio in 1897. She was raised there until she journeyed to Vermont to attend college when she was eighteen years old. It was at the University of Vermont where she met her future husband.

Corinne's husband became president of a big gas company in New York City. She embarked on a new and unfamiliar life complete with household staff: maid, nanny, cook and chauffeur. She had two children and became actively involved in New York society, volunteering for many charitable organizations.

Her happiest times, however, were summers in Wilmington, Vermont, where she and her husband had bought and restored a big house that had once been a stagecoach stop. Eventually, they turned it into a farm. Corinne's husband had been born and raised in Wilmington in an old farmhouse without central heat. He often commented that when he was young, it was so cold in the house in the morning that he and his brother could see their breath. He had not come from wealth but was a self-made man. There were no maids, cooks, chauffeurs or nannies during their summers in Vermont, and Corinne and her husband felt in their element. It was to the farm in Vermont that they retired and where their grandchildren found their happiest memories.

"After my mother and father divorced," Sue said, "it was really Nana who raised me. She was really my mother as far as I was concerned. From the time I can remember, it was Nana who took care of me. When we were in school, it was Nana who cooked our breakfast and got us ready for school in the morning, and it was to Nana's apartment that we returned after school. She was the most loving, patient woman I have ever known.

"After my grandfather retired, he worked for the Vermont Public Service Board. They lived in Barre, Vermont, after my parents divorced. I was five and my brother was two. My mother, brother and I lived with them. When we moved to an apartment, my grandparents moved to an apartment across the street. We spent every summer with my grandparents on the farm in Wilmington.

"We would leave for Wilmington as soon as school got out and would spend the entire summer with my grandparents. My cousins would often be there, as well, and Nana would take care of all six of us. She expected us to behave, and we did. There was a wonderful brook at the end of the pasture that we would dam up and make into a swimming hole. We'd swim there all summer. She trusted us. We had freedom and the responsibility of that freedom.

"We also had chores that we were expected to do. Nana would give us a list at the beginning of the week and would expect us to have them done by Friday. We might wait until the last minute, but we always did them. We painted the porch more times than I can count, weeded her beautiful flower beds, cut back the raspberry bushes, and did other typical farm chores.

"Nana was unbelievably patient with us. Most of the time, we'd make a big mess in the barn in Wilmington. We would make trailers with bedrooms and living rooms out of blankets and use a wheelbarrow as a bed. She'd bring us blankets and linens and we'd play there for hours. She'd come out and have tea with us. Outside my grandparents' apartment in Barre was a landing with a rail around it. We'd make offices there; she'd give us tables and chairs.

We'd make a huge mess with the understanding that when we were all done, we'd put everything away, and we always did. She never rushed us."

It is not her parents' divorce that is the focus of Sue's early memories, rather Nana's sitting with her arms around her on the cot in the corner of the huge kitchen in Wilmington; the sun streaming in the window; her grandmother tucking her into bed at night and reading her a story; getting into bed with Nana in the morning; playing checkers, Sorry, and double Solitaire with her in the evenings; and Nana patiently taking care of her when she had the chicken pox.

"She was also a wonderful great-grandmother to my children. She found out that she had cancer, which killed her, when I was pregnant with my oldest child. Yet she worried about me and took care of me. She lived to see my second child, Scott. He was a baby when she died. I vividly remember the last Thanksgiving she was alive. She was skin and bones by that time, yet never complained. She lovingly and patiently held Scott for the entire meal. As sick as she was and as much pain as she was in, she wanted to take care of him. She went into the hospital at the very end. I was visiting and talking with her two hours before she died. Much of the person I am is because of her. Nana was the center of my world."

Returning Patience to Our Lives

There is a way that nature speaks, that land speaks.
Most of the time we are simply not patient enough,
quiet enough, to pay attention to the story.

—LINDA HOGAN

Develop Awareness

- Be aware of the times you were impatient this week and write each instance in the Patience section of your "Values Journal." What was your body telling you? What did you tell yourself in each instance? Learn to recognize the signs. Ask yourself, "Why was I impatient? What is the outcome I fear if I don't hurry?"

Let Go of Control

- Often the root of impatience is control. Somehow we have developed the mistaken belief that we are in charge of the universe or that we, in fact, should be. The need to control usually masks other feelings. In the Patience section of your "Values Journal" make lists of "what I can control" and "what I can't control." Then list the feelings that come up when you feel that you are not in control. For instance, I am not in control of how fast the traffic moves. The feeling that comes up when I'm stuck in traffic is impatience, and what is underlying it is helplessness. (Usually, the feeling of helplessness has little to do with the traffic and more to do with what you are feeling in your life.)

Adjust Your Expectations

- Sometimes unreasonable expectations can be the basis for impatience. Examine the times this week when you have been impatient. Ask if the expectations you had of yourself, others or situations were reasonable. If your expectations were not reasonable, learn to change them. For example, it is not reasonable to expect a four-year-old to be "neat and tidy" when playing. What is reasonable is to ask the children to help clean up when they are finished with a project or to play with one set of toys at a time. It is not reasonable to assume that you will never make a mistake. We all make mistakes, and a reasonable expectation is to learn from the mistakes we make. Rather than being ashamed of them, learn to celebrate them as gifts of learning from the Creator.

Responsibility

Dr. Miller says we are pessimistic because
life seems like a very bad, very screwed-up film.
If you ask, "What . . . is wrong with the projector?"
and go up to the control room, you find it's empty.
You are the projectionist, and you should
have been up there all the time.

—Colin Wilson

Blaming has become a national pastime: one generation blames another, political parties blame each other, the rich blame the poor, the poor blame the rich, the middle class blames everyone, employers blame their staff, co-workers blame each other and their employers, and everybody blames "the government." Adults and children are not responsible for their behavior because they have one disorder or another or eat too much sugar. Joe couldn't turn in his assignment this morning "because the dog ate his homework." In a 1999 Shell Oil Company poll of 1,277 adults nationwide conducted by Peter D. Hart Associates, 39 percent of those surveyed said there is "a tendency in our society to blame others instead of taking personal responsibility."

The blame game is quite portable and can be played anywhere. The objective of the game is quite simple: to be better than your opponent at searching for enemies and more adept at finding excuses for problems, mistakes, behaviors, feelings or outcomes. Unfortunately, winning the blame game is actually losing. Blaming, instead of being responsible and accountable, can leave us without the power to change. Without the power to change, we become powerless victims, enslaving ourselves.

Responsibility's child is respect. The best years of our lives are often the ones in which we are accountable for ourselves, know we have the freedom and responsibility of choice, and realize that we have the ability to change. Sidney J. Harris once said, "We have not passed that subtle line between childhood and adulthood until we . . . have stopped saying, 'It got lost,' and say, 'I lost it.'"

Young people feel respected when their role models entrust them with important tasks. When they follow through with the given task, they feel self-respect. When we risk being responsible, our reward is self-worth.

Imagine a world where we all take responsibility for what we feel and say, accept responsibility for the environment, our commitments and choices, the children we raise, the elders in our families and communities, and our actions and behaviors. In reality, the decision to create such a world belongs to each one of us. Each of us is ultimately responsible for our own choices.

A few weeks ago, I read a story that spoke to personal choice and responsibility. The story is about a grandmother telling her grandson about two wolves that live inside her. One wolf is white and the other is gray. "The white wolf is good and does no harm, lives in harmony with others, and does not take offense when no offense is intended. The white wolf will fight only when it is right to do so and in the right way. The gray wolf is full of anger. The littlest thing will cause a fit of temper. The gray wolf fights everyone for no reason and blames everyone for its anger. Its anger hurts others and changes nothing. 'It is difficult to live with two wolves inside me, for both try to dominate my spirit,' the grandmother said as the boy listened. Then he asked his grandmother, 'Which wolf usually wins, Grandmother?' His grandmother smiled at her grandson and gently replied, 'The one I feed'"(Giles-Sims).

"Gram" Margaret Goble

I believe that every right implies a responsibility;
every opportunity, an obligation;
every possession, a duty.

—John D. Rockefeller Jr.

Suzanne was packing up her grandmother's things. Her "Gram" was in the later stages of Alzheimer's and could no longer live on her own. Tears rolled down Suzanne's cheeks as she held one of Gram's treasured possessions. It was a snow globe that Suzanne had made for her when she was in the second grade. The baby food jar sparkled and the Christmas tree that "little Susie" had so carefully glued to the lid seem to wink out at her through the crystal snow. "How like Gram to have kept all the things I made her when I was little," she thought. "Everything taken care of, as if each was a priceless gem."

Margaret Goble told her grandchildren that they were the light of her life. She took special notice of their favorite things, so when they came to visit she made certain to have their favorite foods waiting for them. "I learned that love defies all time and distance," Suzanne said. "Gram lived in New Jersey, and we saw her only a couple of times a year, but she was one of the most important people in my life. We would go down there in the summer, and she would come to be with us in Vermont every Christmas. One of my favorite parts

---

The story of Margaret Goble is based on an interview with her granddaughter Suzanne LaFleche. "My grandmother is always good to me. Her gentle spirit surrounds me and warms my soul."

of those visits was the stories she told about her life. Through those stories, I learned about responsibility. She was one of the most responsible people I have ever known."

Margaret Goble began working when she was only fourteen years old to help support her family. She did piecework at the RCA factory in town. Her father lost everything during the Depression. He had been an excellent carpenter and had built a roller coaster in Olympic Park in Irving, New Jersey. Margaret and her best friend were the only two employees out of a hundred who hadn't been laid off at the factory during the Depression. Barely sixteen, Margaret supported her entire family. She walked three miles to work to save the dime it would cost her to ride the bus. Margaret remembered the breadlines and the men jumping out of windows and felt lucky to have a job. "You just did what you had to do," she told her family in later years. "I was fortunate to have work."

Margaret met a man and fell madly in love with him when she was nineteen. He was a tool and dye maker and kept his job during those difficult years. He asked her to marry him, but she didn't until she was in her mid-twenties because she felt a responsibility to her family. They had barely married when World War II broke out. There was a shortage of food, so Margaret worked all day in the factory and at night in the "victory garden" she shared with two friends. They canned all their vegetables, jams and jellies. She shared food with her family and continued to share her earnings with them.

Margaret had almost given up on becoming pregnant and was considering adoption when she became pregnant with her daughter, Elaine, Suzanne's mother. Then two sons were born. She considered each child "a gift from God" and loved being a mother.

When the war was over, she and her husband bought a house in a neighboring community. Continuing her responsibilities to her parents, Margaret and her husband visited them once a week and gave them money to live on.

When her youngest son was twelve, her oldest son was in high school and her daughter was pregnant with Suzanne, Margaret's husband died suddenly of a heart attack. Margaret was devastated. "When I was young, I used to ask Gram if she thought she would ever marry again," Suzanne said. "She hugged me and said, 'No honey, I have only one true love, and when the good Lord is willing, we will be together for eternity.' I remember thinking, *Wow, that's the kind of love I hope I will have.* I learned from my grandmother that when you make a commitment, you don't make it casually; you make it with your whole heart."

Margaret never forgot the Depression. Although her husband had left her enough money to be comfortable, she went back to work in a factory that made lights for stadiums and airport runways. She made intricate molds out of wax, using a tiny torch. The mold was later filled with ceramics. Margaret was proud that her work was never sent back from quality control, although co-workers were sometimes mean to her because their work was often junked. She took her time and was rewarded for her careful work and attention to detail by being made a supervisor.

After her children left home, Margaret bought a Dairy Queen, which she owned for seven years. "It was like a dream come true for a child," Suzanne laughed. "I will always remember the joy I felt making my own sundaes. We always had so much fun visiting her at work; we'd spend hours playing with the empty boxes in the back.

"Grandma was as responsible and meticulous about her business as she was about everything else in her life. I remember once the public health inspector came when we were there. He went on and on about the cleanliness of the place. I guess when he tested the machines for bacteria, he got the lowest reading he had ever gotten. But that was Gram; when she made a commitment to anything, she gave it her best."

Margaret moved to Vermont when Suzanne was in the fifth grade. By this time, Margaret was becoming bent over with osteoporosis and suffered a great deal of pain from arthritis. She never complained and went about life as she always had. "It was by far one of the most exciting days of my life when Gram moved to Vermont. My thought was, 'I'll be able to see her all the time now.'

"I spent a lot of time with her over the years. It was comforting to know that she would always come and get me at school if I was sick. I would stay overnight with her, and we would spend hours playing cards and having tea. There was nothing I would rather be doing than spending time with her. She was my best friend. She never uttered an unkind word about anyone, a lesson I have remembered: 'Bite your tongue. Don't say anything about someone unless you have something kind to say.'

"I remember one day a young woman backed into Gram's car in a parking lot and did a lot of damage. The young woman was afraid to face her and was shocked when my grandmother was worried more about the young woman's fear and anxiety than she was about her own car," Suzanne laughed.

"How did she discipline you?" I asked Suzanne.

She looked perplexed for a minute, then replied, "I don't remember having to be disciplined. I didn't want to disappoint her. I only remember her getting angry a couple of times and that was with my uncle. She would bite her finger when she was totally maxed out and angry. That was as bad as she ever got. She said she did it so she wouldn't say or do anything she'd regret. Her disapproval was the biggest punishment I could have. I loved her so much that I wanted to please her. I didn't want to see disapproval in her eyes.

"My grandmother expected me to be responsible, so I was. She taught me to believe in myself. She would always say, 'You help me so much,' 'I believe in you,' or 'When you have a vision or a dream, follow it through.'

"It was like children were her whole life. She adored my daughter, Deana, her great-grandchild. I am so glad Gram got to know her before her disease got really bad," Suzanne said with tears in her eyes. "It was so painful when she got Alzheimer's. It's like losing her a little at a time. Even though she has such a debilitating disease, she's always nice to everyone and always lets us know she appreciates everything we do. I have never known her to be unkind, even now. I am so grateful that she has been such a big part of my life. I don't think a day goes by that I don't think of all the life lessons she has taught me," Suzanne said, tightly holding the snow globe she had made for her Gram so long ago.

Margaret Mary Goble died at the age of ninety-three from the devastating effects of Alzheimer's.

Becoming More Responsible to Yourself and Others

Somewhere along the line of development we discover what we really are, and then we make the real decision for which we are responsible. Make those decisions primarily for yourself, because you can never really live anyone else's life, not even your own child's. The influence you exert is through your own life and what you become yourself.

—Eleanor Roosevelt

Pay Attention to How Many Times You Blame Others

- Carry a small notebook around with you for the next week. Write down every time you catch yourself blaming others for your mistakes, decisions, feelings and behavior or for the state of the world around you. Blaming can become a habit. Write each instance of blaming in the Responsibility section of your "Values Journal." After each occurrence, write your responsibility in the mistakes, decisions, feelings, behavior and so on.

Empower Yourself and Break the Victim Cycle

We are victims when we are small children or the victims of emotional or physical violence, robberies and so on in adulthood. It is important to be aware of when we truly are victims and when we are not, yet feel victimized.

- In the Responsibility section of your "Values Journal," write down an incident when you were victimized. For instance, as a small child you may have been the target of a bully, or as an adult you may have been robbed. Write your feelings regarding this incident. What did it feel like to be a victim?

- Next, write about a time when you felt like a victim although you really weren't. For instance, you were bullied at work and didn't do anything about it. What could you do to empower yourself and take yourself out of the victim role?

(The above exercise is based on one created by Rod Jeffries. Rod is a consultant for Ancestral Visions and lives in Ontario, Canada.)

Help the Teens in Your Life Become More Responsible

Sometimes we support irresponsibility in youth without being aware of it. One way we do this is to give them money that they have not earned or close our eyes to their irresponsible spending.

- In a household, everyone is responsible for doing his or her part. Expect your children to be responsible and allow them to learn from logical consequences when they are irresponsible. Part of our job as role models is to prepare youth for living in the world. Give your teens a specific amount of money each month that they are responsible for. This sharing is of course based on their responsibility to the family unit. Make certain that they have jobs every week that contribute to the family: washing the dishes, mowing the lawn and the like. They are responsible for budgeting the money they have been given, including saving for things that are important to them. If they run out of money before the end of the month, don't give them more or allow them to borrow on next month's allowance. For instance, if they have spent all their money and want to purchase a gift for a friend's birthday, allow them to be accountable for having spent the money and don't give them more. Perhaps they will have to make a gift or do a service for their friend instead.

Warmth and Humor

A clown is like an aspirin, only
he works twice as fast.

—Groucho Marx

Without exception, two of the most endearing qualities of the grandmothers in this book are their warmth and humor. Our grandmothers recognized all along what scientists are only now beginning to prove; no matter how difficult life is at any given time, there are few medicines that can compete with a good belly laugh. An elderly grandmother once told me that we need laughter along with our tears and that she thought sometimes the inability of some to recover from illness was, at least in part, due to the "terminal seriousness" of health professionals.

Norman Cousins, an American essayist, perhaps went further than anyone, other than maybe our grandmothers, in personally finding the correlation between laughter, which he referred to as "inner jogging," and the healing process. In his own recovery from a serious illness, he found that laughter not only caused a decrease in what had come to be constant physical pain, but also began to turn the tide in what had been a debilitating illness.

Scientific study, although sparse, seems to bear out Cousins's personal experience and our grandmothers' wisdom that a sense of humor not only enriches life but promotes emotional and physical health. One study found that "coping humor" in breast-feeding mothers related to decreased upper respiratory infections in their infants (Dillon and Totten, 1989). Other studies indicate that individuals with a sense of humor have stronger immune systems and better health.

Humor allows us to step outside ourselves, even for a moment, in order to gain perspective on a situation. Sometimes when I am working in communities with extremely agonizing issues, there is so much emotional pain in the room that the spontaneity in the group falls to the basement. Grandmothers have taught me that at these times it's good to bring in laughter or what many First Nations or Native Americans call "coyote medicine." As we laugh, the spontaneity in the room returns, and we can continue our work.

Many individuals who have suffered from physical and emotional trauma have told me that their sense of humor allowed them to endure what seemed unendurable. They somehow had the ability to see their lives in a broader perspective, to stand outside themselves for a brief time, and understand that they could get through the pain. That brief "knowing" was a vehicle for releasing tension, stress and discomfort in a safe way. Then they are able to move from a sense of powerlessness to power and freedom. In his book, George Vaillant lists humor as one of the four healthy styles of coping, which contributes to the continued development of the individual: "Humor is one of the truly elegant defenses in the human repertoire. Few would deny that the capacity for humor, like hope, is one of mankind's most potent antidotes for the woes of Pandora's box." (*Adaption to Life*)

"Grandma" Diane Margaret Laut

A person without a sense of humor
is like a wagon without springs. It's jolted
by every pebble on the road.

—Henry Ward Beecher

At age thirty-six, Diane Laut was shocked to find out that she was pregnant with twins. Diane had three other children, ages sixteen, fourteen and ten, and thought that her childbearing years were over. Her children in school, she had reentered the workforce and had a wonderful job in, of all things, an OB-GYN's office. As with everything else in her life, Diane took this new development in stride, and nine months later gave birth to eight-pound,

---

The story of Diane Margaret Laut is based on an interview with her granddaughters Marissa Baker and Cassie Kenworthy. Marissa and Cassie write "We are both living in the State of Washington and going to school. We thank our grandmother for the gifts of love, compassion, and the encouragement to believe in ourselves."

eight-ounce Billy and seven-pound, six-ounce Andrea.

One day when the twins were toddlers, Diane was getting dressed for work while the twins were busy playing. She had just taken off her clothes when she heard laughter outside the upstairs window and realized that Billy, always a handful, had climbed out on the roof, closely followed by Andrea. Diane climbed out the window after them. After she had gotten the twins safely inside, she roared with laughter at the image of herself, crawling totally nude across the roof in full view of the neighbors. The next day, a "For Sale" sign appeared on the front lawn of the house across the street. With her warm laughter that was known to "light up a room," Diane explained to friends that it had probably been her nude image on that roof that had caused her neighbor to put his house up for sale.

Now seventy years old, Diane's warmth and humor brightens the lives of her eleven grandchildren. "Grandma's laughter is so infectious that it makes everyone around her laugh," said sixteen-year-old Cassie. "When she tries to tell a joke, she can never get through it without cracking up. She laughs so hard that we all laugh before we even know the joke."

"She's so much fun," twenty-one-year-old Marissa laughed. "She seems young even though she's seventy years old. I will never forget the time that we convinced Grandma to go tubing. As soon as she jumped onto the tube behind the boat, we let her fly. With many seventy-year-old grandmas, you would probably just putt-putt-putt along the water, but with her we put the pedal to the metal and away we flew! The boat went faster and faster. She flew left and right as the boat whipped around her. The look on her face was priceless. She was having the time of her life as all of us grandkids watched and laughed hysterically. She was laughing just as hard and screaming at the top of her lungs. The boat took a sharp turn, and all of a sudden the tube flipped, causing Grandma to fly off into the cold water. Knowing her as we do, it was no surprise that she was ready to go again. She lost a diamond earring, but she is not one to complain. Grandma always says, 'It is the memories that make life enjoyable.' She loved it, and so did we."

From the time they were small, Diane's grandchildren loved to come to Grandma's. There was a huge box of dress-up clothes. She always had things planned for them, and there was never a dull minute. "We'd play all day. She always cared that we were having a good time, and she'd play right along with us," said Marissa. "She used to let me put makeup on her, and she'd wear it and the dress-up clothes all day."

All of her grandchildren fondly remember making gingerbread houses with their grandma every holiday season. She ate the candy decorations with them and never complained when there wasn't enough candy left for the houses they so carefully constructed. They always made a big mess, but Diane didn't care. They just cleaned the mess up later. She always told her grandchildren that having the family together was the best part of holidays. It wasn't the gifts that were important, it was the time they all spent making memories.

"Some of my wonderful memories of my grandma are family trips to our river property," said Cassie. "I remember one night we were all sitting around the campfire. Some of us were on chairs and some on logs, but my grandma, grandpa and two family friends were sitting with my brother, Chad, at the picnic table. Everyone was having a good time. All of a sudden, Chad jumped up, and the picnic table flipped over, causing Grandma, Grandpa and their friends to land on their backs on the grass. All of their dinner was on top of them and candle wax was everywhere. We were all laughing so hard; we couldn't believe it happened. Grandma was laughing so hard that she got stomach cramps." For some it would have been a catastrophe, but for Diane it was just one more loving memory.

"My grandma taught me to laugh off the embarrassing moments, because then they don't seem so bad. During the summer of 1997, we took a trip to New York City. Grandma got dressed in such a hurry one day that she forgot to button up her blouse. When she took off her jacket on the subway, her blouse blew right open, giving everyone on the subway quite a show. Together we laughed so hard we cried," Marissa said. "Another time we were at a fancy restaurant, and Grandma had to go to the bathroom. She came out trailing toilet paper behind her, unaware that it hadn't torn off the roll the way it should. She was dragging it behind her. When someone told her, she just laughed that wonderful, infectious laugh of hers, and everyone in the restaurant laughed with her."

Diane's grandchildren said she was their very best friend. They could count on her to be there for them no matter what was happening in their lives. She was always there to cheer them on in their sporting events or dance recitals. She was there for the fun times and for the sad times. "I remember when my parents got a call at midnight one night saying that my dad's dad, Grandpa Doug, had just had a heart attack," Cassie said. "When my dad tried to find his mom, he couldn't because she was at my great-grandma's house. My dad got a double whammy that night. Both his father and grandmother died. My parents went to the hospital, and my brother and I stayed home with Grandma Diane. She came to the house right away to stay with us and comfort us. She hugged and kissed us all night and told us everything would be all right. As always, she made it better for us.

"She's the kind of person who thinks of others before thinking of herself. She's always checking up on friends and family to make sure they are all right. Anyone who meets my grandma would say the same thing, whether it was family, friends, people at church or someone who just met her five minutes ago."

Both of Diane's granddaughters said she was their role model and best friend. "I could tell her anything in the world, and she would give me her honest opinion," Cassie said.

"My grandmother has always been a strong woman with a huge heart, which is helping me shape the woman that I want to be someday," Marissa said. "She's so good-hearted and so funny that she makes everyone around her feel good. She has showered us with love and hugs our whole lives. One thing about my grandma that I hope to have at her age is her warmth and sense of humor. She never lets anything get her down. She always knows how to bring life to a room with a little laughter. Not everyone has this gift. She uses it well because people can't be around her very long before they have smiles on their faces."

Filling Your Heart with Laughter

Any fool can make things bigger, more complex, and more violent. It takes a touch of genius—and a lot of courage—to move in the opposite direction.

—Albert Einstein

Take Time for Laughter

- Make a commitment to yourself to rent a comedy video once a week for the next eight weeks. Invite family and/or friends to share this "movie night" with you. Take note of how your body feels after a night of laughter. Also, become aware of how laughter shared with others brings people closer.

From a Distance

Sometimes when my late husband and I would have one of those ridiculous fights where we were both swimming in a pool of stubborn silliness, I would force myself to mentally stand outside myself and watch myself. Sometimes from a distance, I was able to see the humor in my own behavior, and I would crack up laughing. My husband would do the same thing. Sometimes those arguments are a way of releasing stress. Humor is much more fun.

- Think of a time when you were able to laugh at your behavior. How has it helped you make a shift and allowed for more balance in your life? Write the incident in the Warmth and Humor section of your "Values Journal."
- The next time you find yourself taking yourself too seriously, try mentally standing outside yourself, and look at yourself from another perspective. See if you can spot the humor in your behavior. Write about your experience in your "Values Journal."

Tolerance

Tolerance implies respect for another person,
not because he is wrong or even because
he is right, but because he is human.

—John Cogley Commonweal

Many years ago when I was in graduate school, I was having dinner before class with classmates at a little café near our college campus. We were in the midst of one of those serious conversations about saving the world that young adults in their late twenties enjoy, when a young woman came in with a small child. She was gripping her child's hand and seemed to be having difficulty walking. She was obviously drunk. Soon, everyone in the café was staring at her and whispering behind their hands. The young woman was grasping the counter for all she was worth, while trying to make the waitress understand what she wanted. She slurred her words and was obviously having difficulty focusing. The waitress, for her part, was none too kind, sighing frequently and giving superior knowing looks to the other customers.

Joan, one of my classmates, whispered unsympathetically, "Can you believe her? Totally sloppy drunk. I think they should make you get a license to be a mother! She should have that child taken away!"

I had been raised by alcoholic parents, and the scene in the restaurant was painfully all too familiar to me. I got up to offer the young woman and child some assistance just as Susan, another classmate, had the same idea. "She lives down the street from me," she said. "She's been struggling for a while, really hurting over the death of her mother." Susan had shared that she was a recovering alcoholic in one of their class discussions and had just celebrated her sixth year of sobriety.

Joan commented as we left the table, "You two are something else. There's a policewoman over there. Why don't you let her handle that drunk?"

I helped the little boy with his juice, and Susan helped the young woman with the order. Susan spoke to the policewoman, whom she knew, about making sure that the young woman got safely home with her child. She knew the young woman was living with her sister, and after some effort acquiring her phone number, called to make sure her sister was home.

Throughout dinner, Joan couldn't stop being critical of the young woman, which surprised me at the time. I learned later that Joan, too, had struggled with addictions for many years.

Our intolerance toward others is often a reflection of how we feel about ourselves. Susan was secure in her sobriety, and I had worked hard at coming to grips with my alcoholic family. My parents had died years earlier. Joan, however, was not secure in her sobriety or abstinence and relapsed again shortly following our graduation. Those secure in their spiritual beliefs are tolerant of the beliefs of others; those secure in their sexuality are tolerant of the sexual orientation of others. Fear and lack of knowledge are the root causes of intolerance.

Tolerance is acceptance of the views, beliefs and cultural identity of others. It is the acceptance and appreciation of the differences in others: traditions, cultures, languages, spiritual beliefs and so on. It is acceptance of others' rights to have and express their truths. Having tolerance does not imply passivity or indifference, but rather understanding and compassion for self and others. It does not imply agreement with others' points of view, but rather respect for others' rights to their beliefs. John F. Kennedy said, "Tolerance implies no lack of commitment to one's own beliefs. Rather it condemns the oppression or persecution of others."

Tolerance allows us to work together, have respect for self and others, cooperate, enjoy and celebrate the success of others, and fully appreciate the worth and dignity of the human family.

"Kutsa"
Susie Chief Williams
(Alimpa?ay)

Tolerance . . . is the greatest gift of the mind; it requires the same effort of the brain that it takes to balance oneself on a bicycle.

—HELEN KELLER

As a small boy, Albert was a free spirit. He loved running around the land surrounding *Kutsa's* (maternal grandmother's) house. Early one morning he was busy exploring when he heard the sound of someone crying. The sound was coming from the bathing area behind the woodshed. It was a quiet, peaceful area where he had often gone to sit quietly, think and imagine. When he walked by, he saw Kutsa sitting back there crying. He went to sit with her and began to cry with her. It wasn't until many years later that Albert realized that his grandmother had been grieving that day for her son who had been killed in World War II. He had been flying a B-24 that was shot down over Germany. His body had been sent home in a sealed casket; the family had not been allowed to open it. His grandmother, now a Gold Star Mother, would go to that quiet place behind the shed many mornings to grieve for her son.

"Kutsa was the one who taught us to grieve in the morning before the sun reaches halfway across the sky (noon). This is the

---

The story of Susie Chief Williams (Alimpa?ay) is based on an interview with her grandson and granddaughter, Albert and Veronica Redstar. "Our grandmother was our first spiritual teacher. We will always remember her lessons well." Albert is currently working to restore the Nez Perce language and Veronica is working for Head Start at the Collville Reservation.

traditional lesson about grieving sent down through generations in the Nez Perce culture and a lesson taught by the elders in our longhouse," Albert said.

Kutsa also went to the swimming area early in the morning to grieve the loss of the homeland of her people in the Wallowa Valley. It had become a resort area and a tourist attraction, especially in the summer months. The Nez Perce had long since been relocated by the government to Idaho or to the Okanagan Valley in Washington State where Kutsa now lived. She mourned the memory of the fertile valley; the rich pastureland; the elk, deer and buffalo; the sparkling lakes and streams; the beautiful mountains; and the places her ancestors would go to catch salmon and collect roots for their feasts. She mourned the people who died on the trail with Chief Joseph, her great-uncle. She had loved him and had often shared a big tent with him along with her large extended family at the campsites. He had given her many beautiful necklaces. She kept her treasures in a secret place. She would take them out from time to time, stroking the soft buckskin dresses, touching the beautiful beadwork and holding the jewelry that her Uncle Joseph had given her. She would weep, feeling a loneliness that defied words.

Despite all that had been lost, Kutsa was never bitter. She took things as they came. She believed in the teachings she had received from her elders that she was never to judge people. She learned that it was up to her Creator to pass judgment and for her to let things be. She never judged or talked unkindly about anyone, but followed her teachings even when her husband left her for a brief period for another woman. When she saw this woman, she would shake hands with her, talk to her and treat her with kindness. She knew from the teachings that the woman would learn one day when the right time came. "Just before we're ready to leave this earth, we again see everything we've done," Kutsa would tell her grandchildren. "We will see all that we have done to help or hurt people. We will witness our kindness and tolerance toward others and the judgments and hurts we have caused others. We will see whether or not we followed our teachings. In order to prepare to leave this earth, we will see with clarity the way we lived our lives. We will all learn in our own time."

Albert and his younger sister, Veronica, knew that Kutsa lived what she believed. They had lived with their grandmother from the time they were small children. Albert was eight and Veronica not quite one when their father suddenly died in a freak accident. Their mother stayed close by in the house they had shared with him, but the children came to live with Kutsa.

"She was always busy," Veronica said. "I remember the smells in the kitchen, starting at four o' clock in the morning and lasting all day long. She would cook our breakfast and get us off to school, and my uncles, who lived with us, off to work. Some days she would make all kinds of pies. When my uncles came home, she would have them deliver food to our neighbors and relatives. She would always be preparing something and giving it away.

"My uncles were hunters and would come home with two or three deer. She'd cut them up, dry part of it and put the rest in boxes to share with our community. She was always working, always sharing with everyone.

"One time I wanted to help cut the meat, but she wouldn't let me touch the knife. My uncle came in and said, 'You know, you should let her start cutting the meat, and if she cuts herself, she will learn how to use a knife.' Kutsa didn't argue with him or say a word. She just looked away and continued what she was doing. She was so patient and so tolerant. She would make work seem fun, so I'd want to do it. She never scolded me for making a mistake, she'd just quietly come over and show me how to do it correctly."

Kutsa never scolded or lectured her grandchildren. She taught them by example. They learned tolerance early in their lives. She took her grandchildren to all of the churches in the area. Guiding them to experience every religion was her way of teaching them about the commonalities in spiritual beliefs. "We learned to relate different ways to our own. I remember going to the Catholic church, Methodist church and a Fundamentalist church," Veronica remembered. "In one church, we were told that the ways of our people, our traditional teachings in the longhouse, was practicing heathen ways. Kutsa listened, didn't argue, just allowed the man his opinion, feeling secure in her own.

"Our grandmother taught us to respect and tolerate all beliefs and to follow the teachings of our people. I remember the big gatherings and the root feasts. Today, Albert and I are traditional, and we, too, follow the ways of the longhouse.

"One memory of Kutsa that I always keep in my heart is the way she quietly and with great strength stood up for what she believed. There was a Whip Man in our community who would come by once a week. When he stopped by our house, he would tell any of the children who misbehaved to get a switch from a bush. Then he would whip them for their misbehavior. Even though it was part of the culture, Kutsa did not want us to learn that particular teaching and would hide us every week when the Whip Man came around. We always thought he was a visitor who came once a week to visit with my grandfather on our front porch. I learned from my cousins and peers that he was the Whip Man. The practice was hundreds of years old and was a way to enforce the values of the culture. Kutsa believed she could enforce the values in a much gentler way."

Kutsa's brothers were all in World War II, as were many of their friends. They came home from the war and began to drink heavily. The drinking on the weekends was much heavier and the loudness and abusiveness to one another often frightened Albert and Veronica. "Again, Kutsa taught us compassion and tolerance," Albert said. "She was gentle with her brothers, and surprisingly, they behaved around her. As a young boy, I couldn't understand why she was being so nice to them. I always wondered why she didn't just kick them out, but she never did. She would make them coffee and feed them a good meal. She had such compassion for the pain they carried, and they were watchful of what they did around her. Kutsa believed that you got back what you put out. Everything eventually came full circle.

"We were told we had many grandmothers: any elder woman was our grandmother. They were kind and tolerant, and many eyes looked out for us. We felt comforted and safe," Albert said. "We are so thankful for all their teachings and especially for Kutsa."

Veronica and Albert said that Kutsa's compassion, understanding, tolerance and the power of her teachings are always with them. "When I think of her, I remind myself of the teachings she left for us—values and skills that are often missing in our world today," Albert said.

"Toward the end of Kutsa's life," Veronica said, "she felt great sadness about the changes in values and the pain that existed around her. She saw many men coming back from the war scarred and alcoholic; she witnessed the painful effects of years of oppression; she saw the culture breaking down. From her porch she'd see people driving drunk on the road that passed her house, coming home from the bars in the town close to the reservation. She would say, 'The road is turning red. We need the strength of our teachings. We need the strength of our teachings.'"

Strengthening Your Tolerance for Self and Others

Everything that irritates us about others can lead us to an understanding of ourselves.

—Carl Gustav Jung

Gifts Learned from Those You Tolerate Least

- In the Tolerance section of your "Values Journal," write the beliefs, feelings or behaviors of people for whom you feel the least tolerant. During the weeks that follow, pay attention to the times when you are intolerant of others. Ask yourself what you are feeling. Allow yourself to see yourself mirrored in them. For instance, if you find yourself intolerant of overweight people, ask yourself what you're feeling when you are with them. When you can truly get in touch with your feelings, your ability to be tolerant of others increases. Intolerance for self breeds intolerance for others.

Visit a Place You Feel the Most Uncomfortable and Stretch Yourself a Bit

- In the next few weeks, visit a place where you know you will be safe yet also will feel uncomfortable—a place where people gather for whom you have felt or shown intolerance or about whom you have made judgments: a homeless shelter, a yacht club, an elder's home, a church or temple, or some other such place. Stay for at least an hour and socialize with people. Once back home, write about what you felt on your way there and during your visit. What changes did you have to make in yourself in order to socialize? What did you learn about yourself? Call a friend and share what you have learned.

Generosity

We make a living by what we get, but
we make a life by what we give.

—Winston Churchill

A number of years ago when I was living in a metropolitan area on the West Coast, I learned a great deal about generosity. Every year there was a "Giving Tree" placed in the center of one of the largest malls in our area during the weeks between Thanksgiving and Christmas. Cards were hung on the tree, each with the name, sex and age of a child in the community whose family had difficulty buying Christmas presents for their child that year. Beneath each child's name was the gift that the child dreamed of finding under the tree on Christmas morning. Across from the tree was a café where I sometimes ate my lunch. I am a hopeless "people watcher," and as I ate lunch during the holiday season, I watched individuals and families place gifts around the tree. Sometimes people hurriedly placed their gift under the tree and rushed off to continue shopping; some made a big deal about putting their gift under the tree and looked around as if to make sure others were witnessing their offering; other families lingered by the tree and talked with their children about "the spirit of Christmas" and the value of giving. On three occasions, children led their parents to the tree, proudly holding the gift they had purchased with their allowance. One day I actually saw some teenage boys wait until no one was around, grab two cards off the tree, move a distance away, tear the cards into tiny bits, throw the pieces into the trash and walk off laughing uproariously at their cruel prank.

Some people in our culture measure status by how many material possessions they own and look down on the "poor," feeling sympathy, not empathy, for those they deem lower, and feel "pity" for those to whom they give. Others give to secure a reputation of being a "generous," and therefore "good," person. Many give out of fear—in the hope of getting something in return or to "pay back" what has been given to them. Sadly, there are a few who look with disdain at others in need as a way of bolstering their own fragile self-esteem and live life taking and rarely giving. Many wholeheartedly give from their hearts with no expectation of thanks, favors, paybacks or reward, viewing themselves as no higher or lower than anyone else, just a part of a greater circle of life.

Generosity in many ways is a circle, like many other things in the natural world. A fruit tree blossoms and bears fruit; the fruit is eaten, providing sustenance; the seeds are planted and eventually grow into more trees. A mother gives birth to her child, loves her child unconditionally, teaches and lovingly guides her child until one day the adult child gives life and love to his or her own child. A wise saying from the Lakota Nation is "What you keep, you lose. What you give away, you keep."

Giving not only increases the quality of our lives, but also may increase life itself. New research shows that generosity may reduce the risk of premature death. In the study of 423 older couples, "those who said they gave no help to others were more than twice as likely to die sooner than the people who gave of their time helping others" (Feely, 2003).

Generosity includes more than the giving of material things. Taking time to listen, making another feel at ease and included, giving of time and energy, lending a hand, mentoring, giving encouragement—these things are all part of the generous spirit. And as always, though generous people do not give with the expectation of getting something in return, in the circle of life, we most often reap what we sow.

"Granny"
Bertha Leaver Whatmough

He who allows his day to pass
without practicing generosity and enjoying
life's pleasures is like a blacksmith's bellows.
He breathes, but does not live.

—Sanskrit Proverb

Bertha was tiny in stature, only four feet eleven and only eighty pounds, sopping wet, when she married. Her heart, however, was gigantic. She was always knitting. The minute she met a new person, she started a project: mittens, scarves, sweaters, baby blankets or booties. She proudly presented her creations to a new acquaintance. She didn't have a lot of money, but what she did have she gave away. She and her husband were on a budget, and she had an allowance. But she always borrowed against next month's share to buy yarn or "a little something" for a neighbor in need. She was kind, fun loving and down-to-earth. When she was older, she was everybody's Granny Whatmaugh.

Bertha was born in 1909 in Pawtucket, Rhode Island. She dropped out of school when she was a young teenager and went to work at a factory where she tipped shoelaces. She worked there most of her life. She had one sister, Hulda, widowed and childless, who became a second grandmother to Bertha's grandchildren.

The story of Bertha Leaver Whatmough is based on an interview with her granddaughter Keri-Ann Black-Deegan. Keri is a self-employed CPA living in Vermont with her husband of twenty-five years, Ed Deegan, and their four sons. Keri says, "Although Bertha has been gone for more than ten years, I still think of her all the time and remember her as though we spoke yesterday."

She married Willard early in her life. They were married for over fifty years and loved each other more dearly with every passing year. They had one daughter, who was the light of their lives. When their two granddaughters were born, Bertha and Willard felt the sun rose and set with them. Bertha and Willard never owned their own house; instead they lived in apartments for most of their lives. Their values were different from many of their more upwardly mobile friends, who focused on buying a house or accumulating material objects and wealth. Beyond having enough for necessities, money wasn't important to them. They always felt they had enough. Instead of worldly wealth, they valued the riches of family, friendship and community.

"They'd come visit me in college," Bertha's granddaughter Keri said. "They would adopt all of my friends, and I was always thrilled to have them visit, which was unusual for a young college student. They would usually visit for a week, and it was a celebration every minute they were there. Everyone fell in love with my grandmother. We'd go out to dinner and dancing, and everyone danced with her. We'd go to places young kids hung out, and my grandparents would come, too. Soon everyone in the place had adopted them.

"My grandmother was a knitting fool, making things for all of my college friends. Whenever she met a young couple who were having trouble getting by, she'd adopt them, share food with them, knit for them and buy them necessities that they could not afford.

"She was so generous that she never kept anything for herself. She was always taking care of others. I had a boyfriend in college, and my grandmother somehow knew he needed food. The next thing I knew, she had given me a picnic basket full of food to deliver to him. When I was little, there was a family who lived upstairs. They had a daughter about my age whom my grandmother adopted. She knitted for her, celebrated her special occasions and became the grandmother she never had."

When Keri was young, her grandparents lived in the apartment above her family. Every Saturday night Keri's parents went out for dinner. One of the girls would stay with Hulda and one with Bertha. Both girls always wanted to stay with their grandmother. Their great-aunt never had children, had lots of rules and was very strict. Being with Bertha was much more fun. "I was always the center of her attention at my granny's house. We'd always have a party. My grandfather had to get up at four o'clock in the morning, so he went to bed early. My grandmother would pull out the sofa bed, and we'd eat ice cream, talk and read comics. She treated me like the sun rose and set on me. She was always there with open arms."

Keri's grandparents had the same values: family, friends and sharing with others. They went out for an inexpensive dinner every Friday night and took their grandchildren and their friends with them. They didn't go on expensive vacations because they preferred to be with family.

"Granny got a driver's license for the first time in her life when she was in her sixties because she wanted to drive her elderly neighbors to their doctors' appointments, grocery store or wherever they needed to go. She taught me how to drive when I was fifteen; first the wheel, then the gas. She was so excited that she had learned to drive she wanted to teach me. My grandparents moved into an apartment for the elderly when I was sixteen," Keri said. "There were many widows down the hall from them, and my grandmother adopted all the old ladies."

Bertha was there for Keri during some of the most difficult times of her life. When she had a fight with her mother, as young women sometimes do, her grandmother "made it right." When her twins were born ten weeks early and almost died, her grandmother was with her. "She was up visiting and went to an ultrasound with me. The OB-GYN found that I was six centimeters dilated, and I was rushed to the hospital in an ambulance. My husband was unavailable because he was out walking some undeveloped land for his job, and we didn't have cell phones back then. My granny was with me every step of the way. She was seventy-nine at the time, yet seemed to have endless energy. She got me flowers that day with a Mylar balloon. She wrote 'BOY and BOY' on the balloon. The balloon has never run out of air. Usually those balloons only last a month, but seventeen and a half years later, it is still on my bureau. Everybody in my family knows the story of the twins' birth, and nobody touches that balloon. My granny always seemed to appear for every major crisis in my life as if she were sent by God.

"When my granny died at the age of eighty-six, my sister was on one side of her, and I was on the other, talking to her, touching her hair, loving her. She had a loving and generous spirit. Her love, loyalty and generosity are part of me. I am fiercely loyal and generous like she was. You can count on me forever just as I could count on her. She died ten years ago," Keri said, "and I still miss her every day."

Practicing Generosity

If you have much, give of your wealth;
if you have little, give of your heart.

—Arab Proverb

Sharing as a Natural Part of Our Lives

Without exception, every grandmother in this book shared from the heart as a natural part of their lives. Sometimes we think generosity involves riches when it really has more to do with a sharing spirit.

- Take the time in your life to lend an ear to someone who needs to be heard.
- Welcome a new neighbor with an offering of food or a plant from your garden.
- Share an uplifting story with a friend.
- Visit an elderly neighbor who is lonely.
- Teach your children the value of generosity. Help them sort through their toys and offer one that has had value to them to a friend. Help them save part of their allowance for an offering to children in need.
- Offer to take care of the child of a single parent who has no family in the area and needs a break.
- Share the vegetables from your garden with a neighbor who does not have a garden.

He who buys what he does not need steals from himself.

—Author Unknown

The old song by Merle Travis laments, "Saint Peter don't you call me 'cause I can't go. I owe my soul to the company store." Michael Hill, a reporter for the *Baltimore Sun,* said if Travis had written that song in 2005, "chances are MasterCard or Visa would be substituted for 'company store'" (Hill, 2003). Americans owe more than $735 billion dollars in credit card debt (an average of $12,000 per debtor), and the United States government, as of April 16, 2005, was $7,792,910,914,063.01 in debt, according to the Bureau of the Public Debt. Each citizen's share of this astronomical amount is over $26,000 and rising. As individuals and as a society, we are living far beyond our ability to pay.

At one time, thrift, the wise and careful expenditure of money, was a necessity. It was also a matter of pride. Today this once-prized value is almost viewed as "unpatriotic." In our grandparents' time, the best client at the local department store was the one who would repay what he or she owed. "Among those American values I was raised to cherish, thrift is one," states M. Sinclair Stevens. "Now that we're classified as consumers rather than citizens, it seems almost unpatriotic to be thrifty" (Stevens, 2005).

In today's consumer culture, the best customer is the one who pays only the minimum required each month. Credit cards often charge 20 or more percent interest when the prime interest rate is 4 percent. Today, credit cards are offered to high school students. Credit is a big industry.

What has happened to one of the foundational values of our grandparents' generation: thrift? For some people, credit cards have become the way to stay afloat, making up the difference between salary, cost of living and necessity. Sometimes a new furnace, a roof, a car repair, automobile gas or heating fuel is put on a credit card. A good deal of advertising is now aimed at children, and parents feel pressured to give their children the same things other children have. Other parents believe, or their children believe, that they are entitled to have anything they want and seem to be incapable of delaying gratification whether or not they have the money. Still others believe that material possessions will finally bring the happiness they so desperately seek. That new car, stereo or shopping spree may cause a temporary feeling of well-being, but is soon replaced by depression and/or emptiness that needs to be "fed" until every credit card is maxed out.

I have learned a great deal from the grandmothers in this book who may have lived through the Depression but were definitely not depressed. Most could stretch a dollar around the block and gave their grandchildren priceless gifts from the heart on a daily basis.

"Grammy" Mary Lou Hudson

You have succeeded in life when all you really want is only what you really need.

—VERNON HOWARD

Everyone loved to come to Mary Lou Hudson's house on Saturday nights. She had a musical family: her husband played the banjo, her sisters and daughters sang, and her brothers played banjos, drums and fiddles. They pushed all the furniture back and danced and sang until the wee hours of the morning. Little Judy, Mary Lou's granddaughter, joined in the fun, too. She'd get a spoon out of the kitchen drawer and pretend it was a microphone and sing her favorite song, "Sentimental Journey," at the top of her little lungs. All of her relatives had taken turns teaching Judy the jitterbug when she was barely able to walk, so she always joined them on the dance floor. After a fun-filled evening of laughter, conversation, music and dancing, everyone left with their spirits high and their stomachs well fed. This was actually remarkable because

---

The story of Mary Lou Hudson is based on an interview with her granddaughter, Judy Piper. Judy, who lives in Hardwick, Vermont, says, "I am blessed with three wonderful children and eight grandchildren who are the light of my life."

Mary Lou and her husband had very little money. But Mary Lou could take anything from the refrigerator, pull it together and make something delicious.

Mary Lou had very little money most of her life, and she did not waste anything: After striking a match, she either reused it if there was enough of it left, or put it in a box by the old wood stove and use it for kindling for the next fire. If dresses were worn out, she would cut them up, neatly fold up the fabric, and use the cloth for aprons or dresses for her daughters and later for her granddaughter. She always carried scissors in one of the many pockets of her aprons just in case she needed to save something. Mary Lou used every bit of the vegetables from her garden, even the tiniest stalk or leaf, combined them with leftovers and made a yummy soup that she served with homemade bread or biscuits the next day. She tore the labels off of jars and used the jars again and again. She was an expert at recycling before anyone knew what recycling was.

"The only part of the egg that I would eat when I was little was the yolk," Judy remembered with a smile. "I'd always dunk my bread in the yolk and leave the white. My grandparents didn't want me to waste it, so one of them would chop the entire egg really fine so that the yoke would run all over the white, and I'd eat it. They wouldn't yell or lecture, but just would make sure that the yolk was over everything, and the white was saturated. I still cut my eggs up like that to this day."

Mary Lou worked in the cotton fields most of her life. She and her husband lived in one of the little cabins that had been supplied for the workers by the plantation owner. She gave birth to fourteen children right there in the fields. She would bring the brand-new baby up to the cabin where there was always an older child waiting, then go right back out to the fields and pick more cotton.

"I'm from hardy stock," Judy laughed. "It's hard to imagine a woman going right back to work after giving birth, but my grandmother did it fourteen times. One of the babies died, though, through complications in childbirth.

"Grammy worked all the time. If she wasn't picking cotton, she'd cook or sew. She fed everyone, and she and my grampa kept a roof over their heads. There was always food on the table, and no one ever went hungry. She made all her children's clothes or bought them at the thrift store and altered them just right to make them fit perfectly. She never had a car, never did; instead she walked everywhere she went.

"I was born in Dexter, Missouri. Shortly after I was born, my father had to go into the service, and my mother needed work. The whole family, including my grandparents, moved to Buffalo, New York, and got jobs in the Chevrolet factory. I remember my grandpa took me for a walk every day. He'd walk, and I'd ride my tricycle. There was a barbershop where all the men hung out. Grandpa would talk with them while I rode my trike back and forth in front of the shop. He'd watch me, making sure I didn't get hurt. There was a telephone pole by the barbershop that leaned, and the joke was that Grandpa made it lean because he was always leaning on it, watching me so I wouldn't go into the street.

"I was always in the middle of everything. I saw my grammy every day throughout my life, and there wasn't a day that she didn't let me know how much she loved me. We were all poor, but I never felt poor.

"To this day I can remember sitting on my grandmother's lap and her rocking me. She had this pin that she wore that I still have today. I remember touching her pin as she rocked me, and I always felt so secure. She was always my comfort zone. I feel her presence today. She taught me to be thrifty, honest, generous and to always have an open door to everyone. She never criticized anyone, was always jolly and never turned anyone away from her door. Grammy always fed others no matter how little she had.

"She taught me that love isn't found in material objects but with people and that you can have a wonderful time without spending a cent."

Becoming More Thrifty: Wise and Careful Spending

You can never get enough of what you don't need to make you happy.

—Eric Hoffer

Educate Yourself

- During the next three months, keep track of everything you spend. Enter every penny spent in the Thrift section of your "Values Journal." Try not to pay attention to what you're spending, just record it. At the end of the three months, total everything up and put the expenditures in categories: groceries, meals out, entertainment and so on. Are you surprised at your spending? Did you find that you purchased some things that you didn't really need or want?

Eliminate Waste in Your Life

- For the next month, pay attention to things you waste: Do you throw out food? Do you take care of the things you have, or do you throw them out and buy more? Do you waste electricity by not turning off lights? Do you buy things you never use? With self-awareness comes change.

Intelligent Spending

- After your three months of becoming aware of what you are spending, make a budget. Be sure to include a savings category and, if possible, a charitable donation category (in time or money). Pay attention to what you are spending in each budgeted area. Ask yourself when making a purchase: Do I need this? Can I afford to buy it? Can I pay for it now, or will I have to use credit? Add the amount the credit will cost you in interest to the price of the item. Do you really *need* it?

- Plan an outing with your family or friends one weekend this month that will be fun and cost no money.
- There is an excellent program to teach children to carefully and wisely manage money, which I recommend. It involves giving each child a set amount of money each month that they will have to manage. The rule is, except for essentials, you do not buy them things or give them extra money. This includes birthday gifts for friends, everything. They manage the budget themselves. The spending plan (found in *Prodigal Sons and Material Girls* by Nathan Dungan) advocates requiring your children to save a percentage and to give a percentage to a charitable cause. They have freedom to spend the rest.

Forgiveness

If we could read the secret history of our enemies,
we would find in each man's life sorrow and
suffering enough to disarm all hostility.

—Henry Wadsworth Longfellow

It was the same day as another school shooting. Jeff Weise, a troubled sixteen-year-old boy, had killed his grandfather and his companion before heading to school where he killed a security guard and five students and injured seven, before turning the gun on himself. Jeff's father had killed himself four years before, and his mother was in a nursing home after sustaining brain damage in an automobile accident. Students in the Minnesota high school where the massacre occurred had taunted him.

Hundreds of miles away in Satellite Beach, Florida, Darrell Scott stepped to a podium in a high school auditorium where he pleaded with students to treat one another with kindness. His seventeen-year-old daughter, Rachael, had been killed in a similar massacre in Columbine High School in Arizona years earlier. He talked about his daughter's love and compassion for others. She had said in a written essay prior to her death, "I have this theory that if one person can go out of their way to show compassion, you might just start a chain reaction." When asked if he had forgiven the students responsible for his daughter's death, Scott replied, "We have chosen to forgive because we know people who do not become bitter and angry. We've been freed up to celebrate her life" (Moore). Instead of remaining bitter, Darrell Scott travels around the country encouraging thousands of students to take his daughter's challenge to treat others with compassion.

Forgiving another is not condoning abuse or unkindness. It is not about the past, but about the present and future. It empowers you to live your life in freedom rather than continually being held a prisoner to the past. Forgiving is not about the action, many abuses are unforgivable, but is about the actor. It is not something you do because someone tells you that you "should," nor is it for someone else. Forgiving is something you do for yourself.

Forgiveness takes time. It requires the courage to feel your emotions, to allow yourself the necessary time to reflect inwardly, to confront the pain and then to move on. Forgiveness is not forgetting, but rather putting the past into perspective and giving yourself the emotional freedom to live in the present and future. Forgiving too quickly is a way to avoid feelings, yet if we wait too long, our rage builds and chains us to the past. An old Chinese proverb says it well, "The one who pursues revenge should dig two graves."

Forgiveness is active, not passive. A woman who is being beaten by her husband remains a prisoner if she forgives the beatings and stays to take more. She can attain freedom in forgiveness only after she asks him to get help or leave, thus allowing her to heal from the pain of the abuse.

Many people who are still enraged and resentful about something that happened years ago often have difficulty moving on. I have known those, for instance, who are still bitter about a divorce that happened ten years ago, never entering into another relationship and holding their children as hostages in the war, continually requiring them to take sides. Their continued blaming and resentment allows them to avoid any responsibility for the demise of the marriage and somehow serves as proof of their injury and their worthiness.

Many are held captive by a painful past because they can't forgive themselves. A woman I once met told me that she had been depressed for twenty years. She had no friends and felt no joy. Twenty years before, her son had died in an automobile accident. For years she held tight to resentment, holding the young driver responsible for her sixteen-year-old son's death. She spent hours with fantasies of revenge, enraged that the driver had lived and her son had died. Her rage and withdrawal from life resulted in the end of her marriage and an emotional distance from her remaining children. Her resentment burned a black-and-white world around her, devoid of life and color. When I asked her what would happen if she allowed herself to grieve her son and let go of her resentment toward the young driver, she said that forgiving and moving on would be like forgetting her son and leaving him behind like everyone else had. Later she sobbed as she told me that the last time she had seen her son she had yelled at him and said awful things to him that she wished she could take back. She had never forgiven herself.

We cannot forgive another until we first forgive ourselves. Many things in our lives are not in our control. Life events that we are powerless to stop, leave us changed. What is in our control and power is allowing ourselves the time to heal the hurts, accept the changes in our lives, forgive and empower ourselves to move on with our lives.

"Floss"
Florence Glassmire

Forgiveness is freeing up and putting to better use the energy once consumed by holding grudges, harboring resentments, and nursing unhealed wounds. It is rediscovering the strengths we always had and relocating our limitless capacity to understand and accept other people and ourselves.

—SIDNEY AND SUZANNE SIMON

Four-year-old Theresa sat cross-legged on the floor, watching her grandmother, "Floss," cut up the comics. In a few minutes, Floss put down the scissors and proudly held up the paper creation for

---

The story of Floss Glassmire is based on an interview with her granddaughter, Theresa Peluso. Theresa is happily married and lives in South Florida. "My appreciation for the wisdom and strength of women grew from the seeds planted during my childhood by a woman ahead of her time. Floss's spirit continues to bring me comfort and guidance in the values she lived and taught by example."

her granddaughter to see. "A hula skirt! A hula skirt!" Theresa clapped her hands with glee as Floss secured the paper skirt around her granddaughter's tiny waist. "Now, I'm going to teach you how to do the hula." Floss said, her bright blue eyes twinkling. Soon grandmother and granddaughter were gracefully moving to the imaginary music of the Hawaiian Islands.

"Floss," as she insisted upon being called, was the center of little Teri's world. Her mother had left soon after Teri was born. When Theresa was much older, her father would say, "Your mother went out bowling one day and didn't come back for four years." Teri's mother had suffered a severe postpartum depression after her youngest daughter's birth and began drinking heavily. "It is obvious to me now that my mother is a manic depressive, self-medicating with alcohol. I think if there had been intervention in those days as there is today, my mother would have been treated and would be all right. Although she came back when I was five, she never stopped drinking. Floss supported my father, brother and me during a painful period of our lives. She did her best to keep us on an even keel. She provided us with stability. It was because of her that I was able to work through the pain of my mother's alcoholism. She taught me that it wasn't my fault. She taught me about love and forgiveness. Floss knew a lot about forgiveness.

Florence Glassmire, Floss, was born in Ireland and came to the United States as a young teenager. Soon after she arrived in America, she fell in love with a man several years her senior and they married. He was in the construction business and made a very good living. He and Floss had eight children in a short period of time. One child died in infancy, leaving two girls and five boys. "My mother was the youngest, and the others were stair steps from there," Teri said. "When my mother was three, my grandfather left

Floss for a much younger woman, and Floss was left out in the cold with seven children in the midst of the Depression. Some of the children had to go and stay with other families, while Floss did everything she could to get her family together again. She finally did. She cleaned houses, did odd jobs, took in ironing and sewing—anything to support her children. What happened to her was terribly difficult, yet she never spoke with bitterness. She allowed herself to grieve the loss of her marriage and move on."

Even through the hurt and humiliation of being left alone with seven children, Floss always allowed her children to see their father and eventually her grandchildren to see their grandfather. She was supportive of their relationships with him, never put him down in any way or said an unkind word about him. She knew that her children needed to have a relationship with their father and were entitled to one. She firmly believed that what was between a husband and a wife had nothing to do with the children. They never got back together, and they never got divorced. They were both Catholic, and their faith did not allow for divorce.

"Floss had a grace about her that I never understood, given the pain she suffered in her life. She was kind and gentle and had a wonderful sense of humor. I remember when she was old and had fallen down and broken her hip, she would do "wheelies" in her wheelchair. She was a character, and she was so kind. I know she felt my anxiety and pain at seeing my mother drink. She made it really clear that my mother's drinking wasn't my fault. She explained that my mother was in a lot of pain and had a lot to work out inside her. She let me know that her drinking had nothing to do with me or my mother's love for me. Her love and understanding prevented my being trapped by my mother's pain. She also loved my father and knew the pain that her daughter had caused him.

When my dad was dying and we'd sit and talk, he would talk about Floss with tears in his eyes. She came into his life and took care of his children when he had an infant in his arms. She taught all of us not to let disappointment or adversity get us down. She made sure that there would always be continuity in the family. She *was* the continuity in the family.

"When I was older, Floss moved from Pennsylvania to Florida with my aunt, so I saw Floss only a couple of times a year. She'd write and call all the time letting me know how much she loved me. She died when I was a teenager. She reached out and kept me on an even keel for as long as she could. She taught me about love and forgiveness. Her support and guidance gave me courage and a foundation that has firmly supported me all of my life. She was in my life for such a short time, yet even to this day there is little that happens in my life that I don't think of her, talk with her and feel her presence."

Finding Freedom in Forgiveness

We attach our feelings to the moment when
we were hurt, endowing it with immortality. And we let it
assault us every time it comes to mind. It travels with us,
sleeps with us, hovers over us while we make love,
and broods over us while we die. Our hate does not even
have the decency to die when those we hate die—
for it is a parasite sucking our blood, not theirs.
There is only one remedy for it. [forgiveness]

—Lewis B. Smedes

Practice Self-Forgiveness

- In the Forgiveness section of your "Values Journal," make a list of those things that you haven't forgiven yourself for. It may be something you did as a child that was beyond your control. It may be something you said to your partner or to your child. Next to each resentment, write how imprisoning yourself in self-resentment is affecting your life. Look at the list. Think of the possibility of forgiving yourself. Write a letter of forgiveness to yourself for those things you are willing to let go of.

Let Go of Things You Cannot Change

- Evaluate how you deal with the things in your life that you have little power over. For instance, if an airplane you are about to board is delayed because of mechanical difficulties, do you rant and rave to yourself or others, or do you make peace with the delay and enjoy your time at the airport? Empower yourself to move beyond things you cannot control by changing the messages you give yourself. Self-awareness and acceptance are important steps to change. Here is an example of letting go: "It's really upsetting that my friend forgot to meet me for lunch. I think I've waited long enough. If I wait longer, I am going to build resentment. I have no control over her actions, but I do have choices I can make in my life. I will leave and call her later to find out what happened. I will let her know how I felt waiting for her and then let it go."

Consider Forgiving Those Who Have Hurt You

- Imagine that you are an older adult at the end of your life. You want freedom from resentments. Write a list of those people or life events that you are still resenting. In each case, think of how your life would have been different if you had let each resentment go. Would you have been freer, more spontaneous, more connected with yourself and others, more affectionate, more vulnerable, more emotional and so on? Remember, forgiving is not condoning or forgetting, but rather grieving, letting go and moving on.

  As you examine the items on your list one by one, allow yourself to feel the feelings that come up as you consider forgiving. Can you risk allowing yourself to forgive? As stated so well by Mahatma Gandhi, "The weak can never forgive. Forgiveness is the attribute of the strong."

1. Consider letting go of the resentment.
2. Allow yourself time to become aware of how the actions of another or an event has changed you or your life experience.
3. Allow yourself time to heal your wounds. Name it. Own it. Feel it. Heal it.
4. Acknowledge and allow yourself to experience your feelings.
5. Take time to accept responsibility for your feelings and actions.
6. Empower yourself to forgive, let go and move on.

Value TWENTY-TWO

Faith

We live by faith or we do not live at all.
Either we venture or we vegetate. If we venture,
we do so by faith simply because we cannot know the
end of anything at its beginning. We risk marriage
on faith or we stay single. We prepare for a
profession by faith or we give up before we start.
By faith we move mountains of opposition
or we are stopped by molehills.

—Harold Walker

I remember, even in the loneliest and darkest times of my childhood, having faith that I was not alone and that someday life would be better. Sometimes, during my parents' drunken parties or during the emotional or physical abuse that seemed like a daily occurrence, I would feel the presence of something or someone standing with me. As a child, I would walk in the woods or sit by the ocean, marveling at the feelings of wonder and awe at the energy and timelessness around me. Or I would sing along as my favorite songs, "You'll Never Walk Alone" or "I Believe," played on the radio. I always knew that the footprints of something far greater than I could ever imagine were beside my own as I walked through life, somehow guiding me and keeping me safe.

To me, the meaning of faith is believing in something I can feel but can't see that will get me through the most difficult times of my life. Because of that faith and the belief in a hurting little girl shown by the elders who came into my life, I am alive and have faith in myself today. As stated so well by Thomas Moore, "Faith is a gift of the spirit that allows the soul to remain attached to its own unfolding."

We now know that faith has a major role in the prevention and healing of illness. Heart disease and cancer improve, blood pressure lowers significantly and life expectancy has increased in those with profound faith.

There are many sayings that allude to the idea that there are no atheists in fox holes or operating rooms. A renowned pediatric surgeon and author puts it this way "It doesn't matter if you're secular or religious, Jewish or Christian, Hindu or Moslem. When your child gets seriously sick, you find yourself plunged into a passionate dialogue with God. . . . I've seen kids sustained through terrible ordeals by their belief in Tinkerbell—as long as you believe in something . . . If you don't believe in anything, you're sunk" (Epstein, 2003, 102).

It is often the child who is afraid of heights who falls and the person who believes that he has more to do here on Earth who miraculously conquers illness against all odds. Faith in ourselves, others, in a Creator or in life itself is what carries us through the hardest of times. It is our candle in the darkness. Having faith is not a spectator sport.

I don't believe we can sit back and wait for something to change our lives or take away our pain, and if it doesn't, blame God, Jesus, the Creator, the Goddess, Buddha or Allah for not answering our prayers while we have been passively waiting. We are not powerless spectators in life. What we believe about ourselves and life is the starting point of our experiences. Through faith, we can become what we believe ourselves to be, have the strength to get through the darkest of times and joyously celebrate life's gifts. Faith is not a fortress against danger nor does it prevent suffering. Faith is a serene place of strength, belief and trust where we can continually feel the energy of our hearts and spirits.

"Granny" Mary Edwards

Every tomorrow has two handles.
We can take hold of it with the handle of
anxiety or with the handle of faith.

—Henry Ward Beecher

Nineteen-year-old Mary knew she hadn't taken the clothes. She also knew, as surely as she knew she was breathing, that everyone she worked with in the department store thought she had. She heard their talking about how she had to be watched. She felt their stares as she worked. She was black, so she had to be the one who had been stealing the merchandise that was missing week after week. It was 1941, and racism was just part of life. There were separate seats on the bus, separate drinking fountains and separate schools for blacks and whites. When she had worked in a restaurant, her husband had to sit in the separate section reserved for blacks. Even separate drinking glasses were set aside for "Negroes."

Mary kept doing her job at the department store, week after week, minding her own business and ignoring the whispers. She knew who was stealing the merchandise; she had seen her co-worker stuff things into her bag. She had faith that everything would come full circle in the end. Then one day the older white lady who had been stealing the clothes dropped her big bag, and that day's stolen merchandise came tumbling out in full view of the

---

The story of Mary Edwards is based on an interview with her granddaughter Michelle Hill. Michelle writes "In dedication to my grandmother, the one who continues to inspire me to have faith in God and to stand firm in following my dreams and aspirations."

other employees. They fired her, and Mary still went about her business as she heard everyone whispering to each other that they were surprised because they were sure that Mary had been the thief. She never let the shame get inside her. She felt proud of herself and the work she did. She retired from that department store after working there for almost forty-five years.

"All along they thought it was me," Mary said, as she related the story to her granddaughter Michelle. "You should have seen their faces when the bag fell. They were watching the wrong person, and I just kept doing my job. I knew what I was doing, the woman knew what she was doing and God knew what we both were doing. I had faith that God would take care of things eventually. Things always come full circle, Mickey; you just have to have faith."

Mary's faith got her through really tough times in her life. She was born in Granville County, North Carolina, in 1916. The family was poor. Mary was the youngest daughter, so she had to help out. When she was young, she scrubbed floors and cleaned houses to help support her family. She moved to Baltimore to live with her sister when she was sixteen and was married at seventeen.

Mary's husband was from North Carolina and had moved up to Baltimore, too. She met him in church and therefore believed he was an upstanding, decent man. She had two children with him before she found out that he had another wife in North Carolina. She left him and raised the two children on her own. "Even though he had hurt her terribly," Michelle said, "Granny never harbored bad feelings about her first husband. She never spoke badly of him. I never once heard her speak badly of anyone. She'd just laugh and call him 'that old stump jumper,'" laughed Michelle.

Mary married her second husband when she was twenty-seven, had three more children and miscarried one. "I didn't find out about my grandmother's miscarriage until I miscarried. My granny supported me and let me know that things happen for a reason and that everything would work out. The year after my miscarriage, I had my baby girl. Granny said, 'Remember, I told you things would work out. God always has a plan even though we don't know it.' She had me look into my precious baby daughter's face and imagine life without her. 'God had to make room for this beautiful girl. Can you imagine life without her? God always has a plan. Have faith; always have faith.'

"I know it was her faith that got her through the hardest times in her life. Her youngest daughter, my aunt Carolyn, perished in a house fire. Her furnace had blown up.

"She was able to get my cousins out, but she didn't make it out. That day my granny gathered us all together and told us how much our aunt had loved us. We couldn't say good-bye to my aunt or view her body, but my granny would tell us to imagine her face in our minds and to know how much our aunt loved us. Granny still went to church that week to pray, grieve, and thank God for the blessings she had and for the time she was able to have with Carolyn. Even in her terrible grief, she sang God's praises."

Two years later, Mary's second to youngest daughter, Barbara, died of cancer. "We didn't know she had cancer until the last weeks of her life. That death was really hard because she left two daughters behind, one fifteen and the other ten. She passed away around the time of her oldest daughter's birthday, and her high school prom was in a few weeks. She didn't want to go to the prom or celebrate her birthday. Granny told her that it was important for her to go to her prom. She also helped her celebrate her birthday and told her that in celebrating the day of her birth, they were also celebrating her mother's life. She was in such grief herself, yet she always supported us and held us up. Even through this terrible time, she still talked about how good God was and the wonderful time she had been allowed to have with her daughters.

"When I fall short, I always ask myself, 'What would Granny do in this situation?' She was made to be a grandmother, and there was nothing I couldn't go to her about. When my mother made me mad, as mothers do at times, I would go to her, and just being in her presence made me feel better. She looked like an angel. She wore her hair in tight curls, and she loved to dress up. I never saw her in pants. She was so beautiful when she was young. She looked like a movie star. She also was fun loving. She went to many parties with her friend, Billie Holiday, when she was young.

"She was a positive person all of her life. I never heard her being negative. She had an open door, and everyone was welcome in her home anytime. She never turned anyone away. She had endless faith and a strong and loving spirit. She didn't dwell on the bad. She just lived her life.

"She even disciplined us in a soft manner. When I would talk about someone in a negative way, she would say, 'Now, Mickey, you know better than to talk about people.' And I'd always say, 'I know, Granny. I know, Granny.' When things would not be going the way I wanted them to go, I would get upset, so she'd always say, 'Don't get upset; everything will work out the way it's supposed to.' Miraculously, it always seemed to. She told me to stand up for myself and speak my mind, never to hurt anyone intentionally with my words because I couldn't take them back, and never to go to sleep angry."

Surrounded by her entire family, Mary died of cancer at the age of eighty-eight. She died as she lived: saying prayers, talking and laughing. All fifteen members of her family were with her, telling her how much they loved her and how grateful they were for all that she had given them in life. She died at the beginning of spring, her favorite season. "It rained the whole day," Michelle said. "It was as if the heavens were grieving for her with our family."

"I miss her so much. I know she is in another place, and she taught me that we will all have to pass through death's doorway one day. I have a necklace with her picture on it that I wear every day close to my heart, and I know she is with me. She's right by my heart. It gives me peace to know she's here in spirit. Until the end of my own life, she will always be my guardian angel."

Strengthening Faith

Yes, I have doubted. I have wandered off the path.
I have been lost. But I always returned. It is beyond the logic
I seek. It is intuitive—an intrinsic, built-in sense of direction.
I seem to find my way home. My faith has
wavered but has saved me.

—Helen Hayes

Faith in Yourself

- Think of a time when your faith in yourself wavered. What were the messages you gave yourself at that time? Now think of a time when pure faith in yourself or your abilities supported you to make a decision or accomplish a goal or got you through a rough time. Write this experience in the Faith section of your "Values Journal," or discuss it with a friend. What are the messages you gave yourself that allowed you to have faith in yourself?

Explore Your Faith in Something Beyond Yourself

- As stated so well by Fred Epstein, MD, "It doesn't matter what you believe in . . . as long as you believe in something." Our belief gets us through some of the hardest times of our lives. Sometimes it is useful to explore personal beliefs with others. Ask friends to join you in reading a book or watching a video that challenges your thoughts, and have a group discussion when everyone is finished with the book or following the video. Some suggestions that have been given to me are *What the Bleep Do We Know!?*, *I ♥ Huckabees* and *The Giver.* Ask friends for other suggestions.

Value TWENTY-THREE

Spirituality

Perhaps it would be a good idea, fantastic as it sounds, to muffle every telephone, stop every motor and halt all activity for an hour someday to give people a chance to ponder for a few minutes on what it is all about, why they are living and what they really want.

—James Truslow Adams

My son's fiance, Sarah, writes in an e-mail from India: "The presence of God is everywhere here . . . in a child's eyes, in the landscape, in a temple, in a church, in the kind spirit of our driver, in the home of an impoverished family. . . . I am touched every day by the kindness and humility that exists here." To me, spirituality is *finding the sacred in the ordinary and treating all living things as sacred.*

As a child, I was reminded daily of the Creator's presence in everything around me: the trees, raindrops, lakes, rivers, streams, animals, stars, whispering winds, tall grasses and in those kind and giving people I met along life's way. As an auntie told me one day when I remarked at the beauty around me, "God didn't make junk, Janie girl. Everything he made was beautiful, every creature, every living thing in this vast universe."

I have always felt a sense of awe in creation. Finding the sacred in the ordinary made me feel the Creator's presence around me. Knowing that even though I was often lonely I was never alone, nurtured me—even during the most painful times of my childhood. Spirituality empowered me rather than making me feel powerless; it gave me a sense of belonging not exclusion. Unfortunately, many times religion is interpreted in a way that makes one feel powerless, not worthy and often excluded.

Last week a friend related an experience that was quite upsetting to her. She had been driving home from work, marveling at the beauty of new snow glistening on the trees and feeling that sense of wonder and reverence one often feels when witnessing the exquisite beauty of creation, when a car pulled into the road in front of her. She noticed that the car had decals advertising various Christian colleges and bumper stickers that praised God. Then on the left side of the bumper was a particularly large sticker with sizeable words that read, SAVE A FLAG, KILL A PROTESTER. She said that she was so struck with the incongruity that it disturbed her. "How can a person who professes *spirituality* advocate killing over a difference of opinion or confuse the value of a piece of cloth with a human being?" she implored. Her confusion echoes that of thousands today who are disturbed by the senseless and seemingly endless wars fought over religion, abuses perpetrated in the name of God, or those who believe that the Creator made only one "chosen" race or who advocate only one way to pray.

A wise elder, Harold Belmont, once told me that one should never confuse "Christianity" with "churchianity." This simple statement speaks volumes regarding many people of all faiths who confuse dogma, judgment and righteousness with spirituality. There are many "religious" people who are not spiritual and many spiritual people who are not religious.

Throughout the ages, many enlightened teachers of all faiths have come to share their wisdom, and we have much to learn from them. If we close our ears and our minds to all but a few because we accept only those who pray in our way, we are polarized in a battle for religious "rightness," or in the belief that God accepts the prayers of only a few. As a result, we miss precious gifts of wisdom and bountiful teachings from the Creator. "However precious a jewel may be, it cannot provide the highest spiritual attainment. . . . It is due to other sentient beings that you can develop great compassion, the highest spiritual principle, and it is thanks to other sentient beings that you can develop bodhichitta, the altruistic intention. So it is on the basis of your interaction with others that you can attain the highest spiritual realizations" (Dalai Lama, 2002, 231).

"Gram"
Lois Frederica Fordham

It isn't until you come to a spiritual understanding of who you are—not necessarily a religious feeling, but deep down, the spirit within —that you can begin to take control.

—Oprah Winfrey

"Gram?"

"Yes, Amy Louise."

"Do you believe in heaven and angels?"

Amy and her grandmother sat there, neither saying a word. Then Gram looked at her with that sparkle Amy knew so well and replied, "Yes, I do. I believe in heaven and angels. I believe that when we are born we each receive a guardian angel that stays with us until our time is up here. Their purpose is to smile and laugh with us during our good times and to comfort us and remind us how strong we are during our rough times. We just need to believe in ourselves and in the strength that lives within us. When our time is up and our work is completed here, our guardian angel is there to walk us back home—to heaven."

"Gram's gifts from the heart nurtured my very soul," declared Amy Louise. Her grandmother was a woman of simplicity, wore a big straw hat, always had a smile, and loved working in the garden

---

The story of Lois Frederica Fordham is based on an interview with her granddaughter Amy Louise Fordham. Amy Louise states, "Family is at the heart of everything; life begins there. I simply miss you, Gram, Dillion and Kaylee, with all my heart. Your teachings continue. All my love."

and making goodies in the kitchen of her trailer, including the homemade apple pie that Amy could count on being under the Christmas tree every Christmas morning. She didn't have much materially, but Gram told her grandchildren before she died that she was the wealthiest woman alive. Wealth was the family that surrounded her, that she valued above all else. She taught her grandchildren the beauty of the four seasons and new beginnings: May flowers and baby fawns in the spring, wild blackberries and spruce gum in the summer, cool crisp mornings and big piles of leaves in the fall, the first snowfall in the winter. "See how it sparkles, Amy Louise?" Through these teachings she taught her grandchildren not to be afraid of change or new beginnings but rather to be open to the gifts and lessons that change brings, that life isn't about having or getting, but being and becoming.

The few material goods that Gram Lois had, she shared with her family or those in need. "Your grandmother was the nicest person I've ever met. When I needed a place, she just opened her door and let me in, never asked a thing, just gave me a place," the woman said, meeting Amy Louise for the first time at her grandmother's funeral. The woman had been the victim of domestic violence and had found a safe refuge at Lois Fordham's home.

Lois Fordham accepted people for who they were, which was a great comfort to Amy Louise. "No matter how much baggage I brought into that trailer, I had the security of knowing that I would be listened to and accepted," Amy said. Gram was known never to pass judgment or say a bad word about anyone. At times, she may not have liked someone's actions, but she'd wait for just the right time after she had gathered all the facts, then confront the person in a good way, without judgment. She would say, "You can't tell a book by its cover, Amy Louise. Always close your eyes and listen with your heart."

Lois Fordham taught her grandchildren many lessons of the heart: to find the beauty and gifts in everything and everyone around them and to be aware of the bountiful gifts inside them. She taught them to nurture the very souls of others through knowing, really listening and caring with every part of their beings.

Through her example, Gram Lois's children and grandchildren were taught to respect the beliefs of others and to value a person's right to pray in his or her own way, that wealth is measured by the family and friends around you, and that nothing is more important than family. She taught them to have faith, learn from the good times as well as the bad and to take life as it comes. She showed them *the sacred in the ordinary* and taught them *to treat all living things as sacred.*

"I have come to realize that even after my grandmother had left us, she has lived on. She made sure that a little piece of her lives on within each of us," Amy Louise said. "She nurtured our very souls."

It is often harder to have faith during painful times than it is in times of joy. Yet in those painful times, the strength of our spirituality can comfort and empower us. Faith does not take away the pain, nor should it. Our pain and grief is a gift, one that offers many lessons. Ernest Hemingway once said that after pain we are often "stronger in those broken places." Faith can give us comfort, offer a glimpse of tomorrow and help to put things in context with the knowledge that "this too will pass."

Lois Frederica Fordham's legacy was her children, grandchildren and their families, who came to Amy's side immediately in response to her recent miscarriage because "there's nothing more important than family." Amy Louise could feel her Gram's strength and hear her comforting words inside her even through all her sorrow, empowering and comforting her as she had always done. "It was meant to be this time, Amy Louise. There is strength in tears, allow yourself to cry. Believe in yourself and know that your guardian angel is with you and will always be at your side."

One evening, prior to the death of her beloved Gram, Amy Louise, her small son, Devin, and Gram had gone for a drive. When they returned, the moon was out in all its glory. Gram turned to Devin, "Devin, do you see the moon?"

"Yes," Devin replied.

Then Devin's great-grandmother said, "I see the moon, and the moon sees me. God bless the moon, and God bless me."

When Amy Louise was grieving over her second miscarriage, five-year-old Devin came to her bedside, hugged his mom and said, "Mommy, I see the moon, and the moon sees me. God bless the moon, and God bless me."

Strengthening Your Spirituality

The ability to simplify means
to eliminate the unnecessary so that
the necessary may speak.

—Hans Hofmann

Find the Sacred in the Ordinary

- Take a time every day away from the TV, computer or your hectic pace and spend it in solitude: walk along a beach or in the forest; sit by a stream, fishing or just relaxing; watch children play in your neighborhood. Attune yourself to the energy around you—the strength of the waves slapping on the beach, the amazing beauty and strength of a spider web. Pay attention to textures, smells, sounds, the twinkle in a child's eyes and, yes, the kindness in the eyes of the elderly man you rarely notice sitting on his porch. Feel the energy around you and the presence of the sacredness in ordinary things that you often never allow yourself the time to experience. Make this time of solitude a priority in your life.

Treat All Life as Sacred

- Respect the faiths and beliefs of those around you. Truly listen to what is being said rather than focusing on what you are going to say next.
- Make every effort to talk with people, not about them.
- Put your cell phone away when walking down the street. Look your neighbor in the eye and smile.
- Perform random acts of kindness without the need for people to know what you've done.
- Be aware of the broader creation: take only the food you need; be aware of the chemicals you use that are poisoning the earth; walk or ride a bike when you can; pick up garbage by lakes, streams or along country roads. Be aware of the

corporations that are exploiting other human beings or the earth's resources, and stop buying their products or using their services.

Practice Openness, Inclusion and Belonging

We are blessed in this world with people who come from many cultures, beliefs and faiths—all have gifts to offer. When you are operating from a foundation of spirituality, you are secure in your beliefs and are therefore open to others'. You can greet people with differing views with an open mind and heart and without judgment. When you are without a spiritual foundation or are insecure in your own beliefs, judgments abound and the colorful landscape of humanity is reduced to black and white.

- Close your eyes, relax your body and imagine a beautiful tree. It has a strong foundation with roots reaching deep into the earth. This tree has many branches covered with rich, green leaves taking in life-giving oxygen, its boughs outstretched as if in prayer. This tree represents the truly spiritual people of the world, secure in their beliefs, each branch a different faith, fellow members of the human family honoring creation in vastly different ways, yet all part of a life-affirming process. Now imagine the same tree, weakened, its roots in search of nurturance on a rocky ledge. Only one leaf-covered branch reaches out, seeking life-sustaining oxygen. When you are tempted to judge another harshly for their culture or religion, think of these trees on the landscape. One represents the solidity of spirituality, the other religious fanaticism.

EPILOGUE

Life is not measured by the breaths we take or the riches we have, but by the memories that fill our hearts and are so extraordinary that they sometimes take our breath away. It is in those times when loving memories are fashioned by powerful role models in our lives that values are born, fed and nourished.

When I imagined writing this book, I thought it would be about the values many of our grandmothers and great-grandmothers lived and taught for generations, which are slowly fading, like old photographs, from their rightful place in our homes and lives. I succeeded in writing the book I imagined and learned so much more than I anticipated.

As these powerful grandmothers began once again to find their voices through the interviews with their grandchildren, I was struck by the strength and influence of the values they lived and taught and the potency of their lives. I thought that I would interview a grandchild about a particular value that his or her grandmother taught, only to find, without exception, that these grandmothers possessed all of the values.

They lived lives filled with grace, celebration, truth and forgiveness. Despite the hardships they experienced, their resilience and determination was striking, and their warmth, acceptance, kindness, gratitude, faith and capacity to love was immeasurable.

Though most grandmothers lived lives of scarcity during years marked by war, famine and the Great Depression, their homes were places where anyone in need of shelter would be welcomed and, upon entering, would find warmth, laughter, sharing and generosity.

In truth, I was left with more questions than answers and more hope for the future than I believed possible. I began to question the "progress" we have made over the past sixty years. We certainly have made needed strides in technology, human rights, psychology, civil rights and the rights of women. Yet, I began to question whether we also have, in some small measure, traded resiliency, cooperation, community and family values for "progress."

As these grandmothers spoke through their grandchildren, I was delighted to share the warmth of their family dinner tables, to join in their laughter as they listened to the music played by their neighbors, and to help pull back the living room rug and dance with abandon. I heard the echoes of stories told as they played games with their families and friends on long winter evenings and wondered, not for the first time, how much television and computers have cut a swath through our families and communities. Our lives today are easier with our TV dinners, fast foods and microwaves, but are we safer, closer and more resilient?

As I finish the last word and you put this book down, I wonder, can we have it all? Filled with the warmth of hope from these grandmothers' voices from not so long ago, I am exhilarated and wonder, can we bring it back? Can we have values and "progress," too?

I believe we can if we share our ideas and talents, cooperate, feel grateful for one another, and have faith. I received two letters recently that strengthen my belief that we can have it all. One was from Samuel Jeffries, a twelve-year-old boy. Both of his parents died of the AIDS virus—his father before he was born and his mother when he was ten. He was fortunate that he lived in a home shared by his grandparents and a loving uncle who, with his grandfather, is now raising him. He writes, "In my life I have learned that life can be difficult, challenging, fun, sad and rewarding. Although I have lost both of my parents and my grandmother, and although it has deeply saddened me, I have never let this difficulty stop me. I have been blessed because I still have the rest of my family to help me along the way and to comfort one another in times of sadness."

I am hopeful because of the strong values that I have seen in those whom I have interviewed, like Samuel, and know that they are now passing along the values they learned from their grandmothers. I would like to end with the second letter sent to me in the form of a poem. So many grandmothers have made a difference in the lives of children. Many of those grandchildren are now raising children. With the baby boomers reaching the age of grandparenthood, imagine the positive energy that can be brought forth to balance the strength of the past with the "progress" of the present.

my meme
my meme was very short and very round.
she always did what needed to be done
like loving me when others were not loving
even to themselves.

my meme lived in her brooklyn flat except when
my mom was so drunk and my stepdad was brutal.
except when i needed her more than she needed to
water and nourish the geraniums she grew in her

sixth floor window. they always bloomed in broken clay pots.
and i learned and i knew in that
child's way of knowing that she grew me up
to bloom like her flowers in brooklyn even
in the darkness of home.

my meme fed us in her russian way—enough
for twice our family—with bagels and lox with
blintzes and knish so full that we raced to the couch
my brother and i with him always winning
to rest up for the sweets the ebinger's square cupcakes and
crunch cake with ice cream.
my meme's russian jewish way of revealing the abundance
in our hearts no matter what the darkness.

my meme taught me many things i couldn't understand
'til now and now i find her in my prayers and in my
dreams I let her know "my meme i am all grown up today"
I hear her say "if you are happy dear then so am i"
i sing to her "my meme how i hope you see me now!"

michelle avidon brook

BIBLIOGRAPHY

Books

Bolt, Carol. *The Soul's Book of Answers*. New York: Stewart, Tabori and Chang, 2003.

Cousins, Norman. *Anatomy of an Illness*. New York: W.W. Norton and Company, 1979.

Dalai Lama. *Advice on Dying*. Jeffrey Hopkins, PhD, ed. and trans. New York: Atria Books, 2002.

Dalai Lama, and Howard Cutler MD. *The Art of Happiness: A Handbook for Living*. New York: Riverhead Books, 1998.

Epstein, Fred, MD, and Joshua Horwitz. *If I Get to Five: What Children Can Teach Us About Courage and Character.* New York: Henry Holt and Co., 2003.

Flach, Frederick C., MD. *Resilience: Discovering a New Strength at Times of Stress*. New York: Fawcett Columbine, 1998.

Janki, Dadi. *Pearls of Wisdom*. Deerfield Beach, Florida: Health Communications, Inc., 1999.

Longman, Addison Wesley, ed. *Longman Dictionary of American English*. New York: Pearson Education. 2002.

Middelton-Moz, Jane. *Shame and Guilt: Masters of Disguise*. Deerfield Beach: Florida: Health Communications, Inc., 1990.

———. *The Will to Survive: Affirming the Positive Power of the Human Spirit*. Deerfield Beach, Florida: Health Communications, Inc., 1992.

Middelton-Moz, Jane, Lisa Tener, and Peaco Todd. *The Ultimate Guide to Transforming Anger: Dynamic Tools for Healthy Relationships*. Deerfield Beach, Florida: Health Communications, Inc., 2004.

Peck, M. Scott, MD, ed. *Abounding Grace: An Anthology of Wisdom.* Kansas City, Missouri: Ariel Books, Andrews McMeel Publishing, 2000.

Running Press eds., *The Quotable Woman: Love and Relationships.* Philadelphia: Running Press, 1991.

Stinnett, N., and J. DeFrain. *Secrets of Strong Families.* Boston: Little, Brown and Company, 1985.

Stokes, John, Kanawahienton and Rokwaho. *Thanksgiving Address: Greetings to the Natural World.* Corrales, New Mexico. Native Self-Sufficiency Center, Six Nations Museum, Tracking Project, Tree of Peace Society, 1993.

Vaillant, George E. *Adaption to Life.* Boston: Little, Brown and Company, 1977.

Wolin, Steven J., MD, and Sybil Wolin, PhD. *The Resilient Self: How Survivors of Troubled Families Rise Above Adversity.* New York: Villard Books, l994.

Periodicals

Bertell, Rosalie, PhD. "In What Do I Place My Trust." The Internation Institute of Concern for Public Health. *http://www.iicph.org/rosaliebertell/trust.htm.*

Block, Cindy Eileen. "College Students Perceptions of Social Support from Grandmothers and Stepgrandmothers." *College Student Journal* (September 2002).

Deegan, P. "Recovery as a Journey of the Heart." *Psychiatric Rehabilitation Journal* 19.3 (Winter 1996): 91–98.

Dillon, Kathleen, and Mary Totten. "Psychological Factors, Immunocompetence and Health in Breast-Feeding." *Journal of Genetic Psychology* 150 (1989): 155–162.

Feely, Richard, DO. "Generosity and Longevity." Dr. Feely.com, Research News 1:1 (2003). *http:www.drfeely.com/patientcare/wh/volume_2003_1_1_b.htm.*

Fitzgerald, Robert. "If Honesty Doesn't Matter, Then What Does?" March 2, 2004. UNIYA: Jesuit Social Justice Centre. *http://www.uniya.org.*

Giles-Sims, Jean, PhD. "Traditional, Enlightened and Empowered Grandmothers." *http://www.grandmotherconnections. Grandmother Connections, com.*

Grossman, Lev. "Grow Up? Not So Fast." *Time,* 4 January 2005: 42–54.

Hart, Kenneth E., PhD. "Research on Humility for Existential Psychologists in the 21st Century." International Network on Personal Meaning (INPM). *http://www meaning.ca/articles/humility_hart.htm.*

Hart, Peter D. "Shell Oil Company Shell Poll." Hart Research Company, March 16–20, 1999.

Hill, Michael. "The Great American Burden: A New Report Shows Rapid Growth in Families' Debt from Credit Cards." Perspectives, *Baltimore Sun,* 28 September 2003.

Jennings, Marianne. "Kitchen Table Vital to Family Life." *Desert News,* 9 February 1997: quoted in S.R. Covey, *The 7 Habits of Highly Effective Families*. New York: Golden Books, 1997.

Keltner, Dacher. "The Compassionate Instinct; Think Human's are Born Selfish? Think Again." *Greater Good* (April 2004): 6–9.

McCullough, M. E., R. A. Emmons, and J. Tsang. "The Grateful Disposition: A Conceptual and Empirical Topography." *Journal of Personality Psychology and Social Psychology* 82. (1 January 2002): 112–27.

McElroy, Wendy. "Muslim Woman's Courage Sets Example." *The American Daily,* 17, March, 2005.

Mischel, Michael. "The Stanford University Marshmallow Study: Delayed Gratification (Self-Discipline) the Key to Long Term Success." Sybervision. *http://www.sybervision.com/Discipline/marshmallow.htm*.

Stevens, M. Sinclair. "Thrift." 13 January, 2005. *Words into Bytes: Life in the 21st Century*. *http://www.zanthan.com/wordsintobytes/archives/001909.html*.

ABOUT THE AUTHOR

Jane Middelton-Moz, M.S. is a trainer, consultant and community interventionist. She speaks internationally on issues of multi-generational grief and trauma, anger, and bullies and bullying. She has appeared on national radio and television, including: *Oprah, Montel* and PBS. She is the author of *Children of Trauma, Shame and Guilt, Boiling Point* and *Welcoming Our Children to the New Millennium*. She is the coauthor of *Bullies: From the Playground to the Boardroom* and *The Ultimate Guide to Transforming Anger*.

Jane is the director of the Middelton-Moz Institute a division of The Institute of Professional Practice, *www.ippi.org*, a large multi-state not for profit human service organization. She lives in Vermont.